THE ENCYCLOPEDIA OF CHAMPIONSHIP WRESTLING DRILLS

THE ENCYCLOPEDIA OF CHAMPIONSHIP WRESTLING DRILLS

Ray F. Carson

SOUTH BRUNSWICK AND NEW YORK: A. S. BARNES AND COMPANY
LONDON: THOMAS YOSELOFF LTD

© 1974 by A. S. Barnes and Co., Inc.

A. S. Barnes and Co., Inc.
Cranbury, New Jersey 08512

Thomas Yoseloff Ltd
108 New Bond Street
London W1Y OQX, England

Library of Congress Cataloging in Publication Data

Carson, Ray F.   1939-
  The encyclopedia of championship wrestling drills.

  Bibliography: p.
  1. Wrestling. I. Title.
GV1195.C335   796.8'12   73-18862
ISBN 0-498-01468-1

PRINTED IN THE UNITED STATES OF AMERICA

To Dean Herbert J. Nelson of San Diego City
College, San Diego, California, and Mr.
Clifford W. Buck, Chief of Driver Instruction,
Grossmont Union High School District,
La Mesa, California

CONTENTS

PREFACE

Here, clearly illustrated with more than one hundred diagrams, photographs, and tables are drills covering every aspect of wrestling. Devised to speed up and simplify the teaching of basic skills, these drills cut coaching efforts to a minimum.

Every kind of drill ever needed is presented. Each is complete with an accurate detailed description.

Included are:

> Situation drills
> Reaction drills
> Series drills
> Conditioning drills
> Game-type drills
> Takedown-escape-reversal drills
> Individual and team drills

. . . and many, many more.

With this indispensable guide little difficulty is encountered in finding drills specific to coaching purposes. It's packed with special drills for developing explosive moves from underneath, capitalizing upon opponents' weaknesses, and maintaining dominant control.

Among the one hundred and one drills shown here, many have never been seen before.

All drills are grouped and categorized as follows:

14 Rotational Drills

These individual-type drills, two- and three-man drills, and full-team drills provide for a variety of wrestling experiences.

20 Competitional Drills

These matchlike drills simulate conditions commonly encountered in the heat of competition.

6 Situational Drills

These drills place a boy in challenging situations that require him to think, analyze, and react.

22 Educational Drills

These drills are designed for gaining mastery over wrestling fundamentals. A boy learns all the necessary mechanics of a championship attack and defense.

8 Sequential Drills

These drills turn skills into automatic reflex actions that enable a boy to take full advantage of scoring opportunities.

16 Recreational Drills

These drills inject new life into routine practice sessions. They stimulate interest and arouse enthusiasm in the wrestling program.

It all adds up to a one-volume wrestling drills library with everything necessary for developing a top-notch wrestling program.

ACKNOWLEDGMENTS

I make no claim for the originality of many of the drills included in this text. Many people have, over the years, directly and indirectly contributed their ideas to the development of these drills. Those originally responsible for devising them are unknown. I am, therefore, at a loss as to whom to attribute them per se.

A variety of literature on wrestling was researched as a means of obtaining ideas for drills. A comprehensive list of these sources appears in the bibliography.

In the preparation of this book, particular thanks are expressed to photographer Clayton W. Beeson. The manuscript was typed by Emerita Lafon. Coaches Mark Whittleton and Frank Barry selected the wrestlers used for the illustrations.

Gratitude is expressed to the following members of the wrestling teams at San Diego High School and San Diego City College for posing for the pictures included in the text:

Carl "Rusty" Arnesen
Bobby Borja
Michael Estrada
Edward "Chip" Gonzalez
Louis McKay, Jr.
Mario Alfonso Montes
John O'Neal
Alfred J. Peterson
Alfred D. Serrano

INTRODUCTION

This book represents the most comprehensive guide presently available on wrestling drills. It is unmatched for solid, usable, and challenging drills covering every aspect of the sport.

With the aid of a variety of diagrams and photographs, one hundred and one exciting drills are provided for developing a championship wrestling program. Best of all, many of these drills incorporate challenging ideas and unique approaches for teaching and coaching the fundamentals of wrestling. Many conventional drills have been transformed by unusual motivating gimmicks and varied patterns.

This book is written specifically for coaches, physical education teachers, athletic directors, and recreation leaders. It is particularly valuable where there is: (1) an inadequate amount of practice space and/or facilities; (2) an insufficient or overabundant number of participants; and/or (3) a limited amount of available time.

An attempt has been made to make this book as useful as possible. Most of the drills included require little or no equipment. A special endeavor has been made to keep the material easy to find. Simplicity and convenience of reference are emphasized. Each chapter has been arranged to accommodate a specific category of drills.

THE ENCYCLOPEDIA OF CHAMPIONSHIP WRESTLING DRILLS

1
PSYCHOLOGICAL ASPECTS OF DRILLS

The more a skill is repeated, the more firmly established it becomes.

Proficiency is dependent upon repetition. The more often a move is drilled upon, the easier it becomes to execute.

The actual amount of practice needed to learn anything new depends upon the level of ability of the learner and the complexity of the task. The higher the ability of the learner and the less complex the particular task, the more likely it is that it can be performed well without a great deal of practice.

Most wrestling moves can be learned quickly. However, it is only after adequate practice that they can be executed with any reasonable degree of success in competition.

There is a natural tendency, unfortunately, to feel that mastery is attained after practicing a new skill a few times. This reaction is misleading since the ability to employ the skill successfully, under the type of pressure evidenced in competition can only be acquired through intensive practice. There is no easy way.

Things happen in wrestling too rapidly for the wrestler to stop and think about what to do or how to do it. Situations are constantly changing. An opening may present itself only for a fleeting moment. Taking time to appraise a situation generally results in a completely different set of circumstances before a decision is reached. In wrestling, he who hesitates is lost.

Wrestling moves must be practiced until they become immediate responses that can be executed with quickness and precision. The greater the amount of practice, the sooner the moves will become established reflexes.

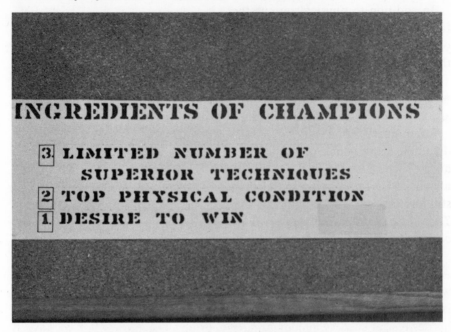

INGREDIENTS OF CHAMPIONS

3. LIMITED NUMBER OF
   SUPERIOR TECHNIQUES
2. TOP PHYSICAL CONDITION
1. DESIRE TO WIN

Initially, the mechanics of performing a new skill are rather awkward because they are under the conscious control of the learner. The learner must literally think out each movement.

A certain degree of slowness or hesitancy accompanies the performance of a new skill. Later, however, with correct practice, the movements become more precise and sophisticated. Through the use of drills, skills applicable to particular situations become more firmly established and can be performed more quickly.

Learning is dependent upon the learner's readiness to act.

There are two basic elements that influence the readiness of a learner to act. They are the learner's (1) state of fatigue, and (2) degree of motivation. A highly motivated and relatively unfatigued individual is generally considered to be in the most mentally and physically receptive state to learn.

The learner is less attentive when tired. He finds it difficult to focus his attention on what he is being told at a time when he is more concerned with "catching his breath." Also, when fatigued, his muscles fail to function in the same manner they would when unfatigued. When tired, larger movement patterns are substituted for finer more precise ones. Consequently, at this time, any attempt to learn something new is likely to result in a sluggish and half-hearted effort.

In addition to physical fatigue there is also a psychological or mental fatigue. This type of fatigue is specifically related to the learner's degree of motivation. He tends to tire more quickly when engaged in something that does not interest him as opposed to something he is very eager about.

Activities that carry little or no rewards, particularly in terms of status or esteem, are viewed as distasteful or unpleasant. They are commonly accompanied by a learner's reaction of excessive tiredness.

Oftentimes, fatigue or a decreased work capacity is caused by boredom. Weariness, lack of snap, loss of interest, and what appears to be an absence of endurance are evidenced. This condition can quickly be alleviated by introducing the element of fun or competition, or by substituting new and challenging activities for old routines.

The effect of an act, whether it is pleasing or displeasing, influences the chances of its recurrence.

Experiences that the learner finds rewarding are likely to be repeated. A wrestler who finds success and satisfaction in an initial experience will tend to repeat that experience. On the other hand, if the experience is unpleasant, displeasing, or unprofitable inasmuch as it does not gratify his desires for success, recognition, and/or accomplishment, it will likely be avoided in the future and its chances of recurrence vastly diminished.

This is the reason why, for example, it is important that a counter to any wrestling technique not be demonstrated until that technique has been at least partially mastered.

Only in the event that the technique is one that is undesirable to use is it wise to show the counter immediately after demonstrating the skill. If the learner's initial experience in attempting the technique is unsatisfactory that experience will discourge its use. He will lose confidence in its effectiveness and consequently it will likely remain an undeveloped part of his repertoire.

The wrestler looks forward to workout sessions that are pleasant and rewarding. Unchallenging sessions are often merely tolerated as prerequisites for competing. Dull, boring, and monotonous routines must be eliminated if interest is to be maintained. If this is not done it could mean the premature termination of a wrestler's career.

2
PHYSIOLOGICAL ASPECTS OF DRILLS

Learning how to perform a particular skill is dependent upon obtaining information about the skill from a variety of sources.

From a physiological standpoint there exist basically three major sources from which information is acquired in learning a particular skill. These sources are visual, auditory, kinesthetic, or any combination thereof.

A skill is learned through the senses. By watching a skill performed and then hearing and/or reading about how it is done, the learner is able to copy it.

Imitation is the most common means of learning a new skill. The learner observes and then attempts to repeat what it is he sees. The coach generally gives him cues regarding what it is he might be doing improperly. This accelerates the learning process since the learner does not have to go through the lengthy process of trial and error to correct his mistakes. By knowing what he must do to get the desired results he can eliminate inappropriate movements.

Most skills can be performed with a reasonable degree of correctness after only a few trials. However, it is only after a considerable amount of practice and time that they can be used effectively in competition.

Repetitive practice strengthens the association between the stimulus and the response.

Neural pathways are composed of three kinds of nerve cells—receptors, connectors, and effectors. The receptors pick up or receive various stimuli from the environment through hearing, sight, and other bodily senses. The stimulus is then carried, in the form of an impulse, to the

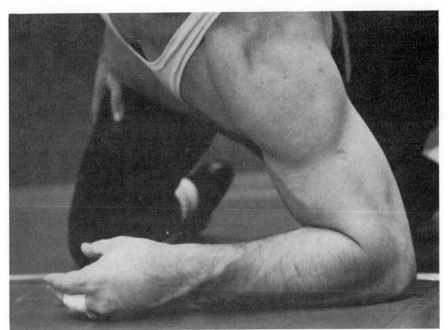

connector cells and finally to the receptor cells. These impulses are electrical and/or chemical in composition. They trigger a response mechanism in the effector cells located in the muscles. The muscles react to the stimulation by contracting, and thereby concluding the sequence of events leading up to the execution of the action.

Learning is a neurological process. Within the neurological system, pathways are established for all movement patterns. The proper movements practiced in the proper sequence and with the proper amount of repetition establishes the formation of desired neural pathways. The more often impulses are sent over these neural pathways, the more firmly established they become. Efficiency increases until eventually the movement pattern becomes mechanical. This explains the importance of drills and the basis for suggesting that practice makes perfect.

Sensory impulses are responded to more effectively and efficiently as the various pathways in the nervous system become more developed. The more often they are traveled the quicker and more precise the movement pattern becomes. Resistance between the stimulus and the response is correspondingly reduced. The nervous impulse will always utilize the path of least resistance.

The bond established between the stimulus and the response is strengthened each time the particular movement is performed. This bond between the particular stimulus and the desired response is further and further developed with repeated practice.

Practice makes the response automatic, thereby enhancing the chances of success.

If drilled upon sufficiently, movement patterns or pathways become so well established that nerve impulses can travel over them without direct control from the higher brain center. In such instances, the skill is executed without a conscious awareness on the part of the performer.

Neurologically speaking, when first starting to practice a new skill, the initial pattern extends from the cerebral cortex directly to projector neurons through the brain stem and down the anterior horns of the spinal cord to the muscles used. However, after a considerable amount of practice a different neural network is formed that is better adapted to this function. Rather than being consciously controlled by detailed directions given by the cerebrum, this other more complex neural network needs only to receive an initial impulse before the skill is performed automatically.

When the response of a motor neuron does not require the direct involvement of the brain, but is instead handled by the spinal cord, it is known as a reflex. Instead of the message going to the brain it takes a short cut through which information passes directly to the muscles, which in turn contract or relax. This is much faster than the delayed, slower, and more complicated process involving thought. Movements that require a minimum of mental contemplations are the quickest to materialize. They are performed with little, if any, reference to conscious thought.

The learner having developed a new motor (movement) pattern needs only a voluntary initiator impulse to have it performd automatically.

Once established the movement pattern is stored in the mind. It can be selected and released when needed. A stimulus is all that is required for the movement to appear. The stimulus sets into motion the necessary nerve impulses to effect the appropriate muscles in such a coordinated sequence so as to cause the desired movement to be performed automatically.

Quickness is best developed through drills. Drills can condition the learner to recognize and anticipate. Time lapses for contemplating an opponent's vulnerability are thereby vastly shortened.

As movements become more automatic, the learner is able to free his mind of conscious efforts related to the detailed movements involved in the performance of skills. This provides more of an opportunity to concentrate on strategy. The more mechanical skills become, the more completely free the mind becomes for planning ways of defeating the opponent.

Efficiency of movement assures maximum certainty of success with a minimum expenditure of energy.

The ability to move is fundamental to the execution of any wrestling technique. But the ability to move effectively is quite different than just being able to move. This ability is developed through practice. When correct movements are practiced in the form of drills, they become physiologically more economic, perfectly timed, and correctly adjusted to produce the desired results.

During the early stages of learning, there exists a certain degree of unwanted bodily tension. While attempting a new skill many muscles are likely to contract that do more to hinder than enhance performance. By properly practicing correct movement, useless and extravagant contractions are gradually eliminated and the pattern is done with greater ease and more efficiency. The more the correct movement is practiced the better it is learned. As proficiency in executing the pattern improves, the number of unnecessary muscular contractions becomes fewer. A reduction in the amount of energy required to perform the skill results.

In order to conserve energy, the level of performance must be high. Skillful performance results from efficient movement. Efficient movement is characterized by an absence of unnecessary muscular contractions. The smaller the number of wasted contractions, the greater the efficiency of movement. The more efficient the movement, the greater the amount of work that can be accomplished for the amount of energy expended. The more work that can be done the longer the performance can be continued. Thus, a harmonious cycle is established whereby endurance is prolonged to the degree the skill is perfected in performing the movement pattern. The greater the skill, the less the energy expenditure resulting from the elimination of unnecessary movements. In the simplest terms, it amounts to doing the most with the least effort.

3
PEDAGOGICAL ASPECTS OF DRILLS

Proper administration of drills is of paramount importance.

Each drill should be introduced briefly and conducted as expediently as possible. It is best to announce the drill, put the wrestlers in proper formation, explain and if necessary demonstrate, ask for questions, and then start. If the drill has been used before naming it will help convey to the wrestlers the formation that is required.

Preparation for conducting the drill should be completed before it is introduced. All timers, stopwatches, and other equipment necessary should be handy and ready for use. Taking time away from the drill to get needed equipment is a mistake.

The wrestlers should be put in formation before an explanation of the drill is given. This makes the drill much simpler to explain.

Some drills will require boundary or limit lines. These lines should be marked as definitely as possible. Confusion over poorly defined lines can ruin a drill.

Arrangements should be made to have everyone participate. If equal-sized groups are to be used in the drill, a count should be taken and any adjustments made before starting. Those who are physically temporarily incapacitated from taking a fully active part in the drill can be used as referees, timers, scorers, and so on. It is better to keep them occupied doing something than to have them idly standing on the sidelines.

An explanation of the drill accompanied by a demonstration facilitates understanding of how it is to be performed.

No attempt should be made to explain the drill until everyone is quiet

and attentive. Unless quiet exists some will not hear or understand how the drill is to be performed. This will necessitate repeating the explanation.

The explanation should be brief and to the point. Long, detailed descriptions are undesirable. They often do more to confuse the situation than they do to aid it. The fewest words possible should be stressed while the lesser details are allowed to take care of themselves.

The explanation may, for the sake of clarity, be accompanied by a demonstration. This is oftentimes far more meaningful than an explanation alone. Some of the more skillful wrestlers should be chosen for the demonstration.

After explaining and demonstrating the drill, it often happens that something is overlooked or not totally understood by the group. It is therefore desirable to ask if there are any questions before going on.

Questions should be answered so that all can hear rather than just the individual asking the question. If one person is uncertain about a particular point, it is likely to also be hazy in the minds of others. *Drills characterized by discipline, order, and good management are the most beneficial.*

A whistle should be used in conducting most drills. It provides the most practical means of gaining attention, starting drills, conducting repeated efforts, and halting drills. The wrestlers should be expected to stop, look, and listen the instant it is blown. Compliance must be insisted upon.

Horseplay should be halted at its first appearance. Favored individuals should never be allowed to get away with it since others quite naturally will follow their lead.

If a drill is going poorly it should be stopped at once and the difficulties corrected. The drill should then be started over from the beginning. Minor faults, however, can often be corrected while the drill is in progress. Whenever possible this is preferable to having to stop the drill.

Successful drills are characterized by activity that is snappy and vigorous. The principal factor is a hustling attitude combined with a spirit of enthusiasm. The activity should be as continuous as possible throughout the drill.

In order to insure continuous wrestling during a drill, the rule should be established at the start that anytime a wrestler is pinned, collides with another, or goes off the mat, he stops and immediately starts again in the same position assured at the beginning of the drill.

Drills terminated before interest is lost and the activity begins to drag are the ones most enjoyed.

Unfortunately, some drills are often overused and become boring and so routinely dull that they are not performed as enthusiastically as they should be. Repetitive use of a drill can make it a drudgery to perform and a morale killer. Wrestlers cannot be expected to be interested in the same drill each day. Day-after-day, week-after-week monotony can deaden fun and enthusiasm.

A drill should never be allowed to drag along after interest is lost. It should be terminated while it is still going strong. In this way renewed interest is realized the next time it is used.

After a drill has been used a few times it may begin to lose its appeal. In such cases, slight variations can be introduced to produce renewed interest and enthusiasm. The drill may be used in this way for an entire season with excellent results.

4
ROTATIONAL DRILLS

The physical arrangement for rotational drills consists of a series of stations or circles located around the mat. Wrestlers are expected to move or rotate from station to station.

All rotational drills include four variables. These variables are as follows:

Variable #1 — Position
Positions of the wrestlers can be adjusted to permit any type of interacting competition desired. Positions such as standing, prone, on one side, hands and knees, sitting, supine, one and both knees are most commonly used.

Variable #2 — Time
A time factor can be interjected into any or all of the stations in the rotational pattern. The duration of efforts can be either informally established or rigidly controlled.

Variable #3 — Intensity
The intensity of effort can be gauged for passive to active resistance. The pace can be set so that the work being performed is anywhere from a slow speed to an all-out exertion.

Variable #4 — Situation
Different situations can be created at each station. Wrestlers can be exposed to varied moves and a variety of circumstances at particular points in the rotations pattern.

These variables are controlled and manipulated as a means of varying the drills and the style of work being done.

#1—*Two-On-One Rotational Drill*

This drill is useful in conditioning the exceptional varsity wrestler. The varsity man competes against two other men selected by the coach on the basis of their combined ability to provide the varsity man with a strenuous workout. These men do not necessarily have to be from the same weight class as the varsity man.

While one man works with the varsity wrestler, the other rests. The varsity man is thereby constantly confronted with a fresh opponent.

		Round I	
Period	*Resting*	*Wrestling*	*Position*
1	3	1 - 2	standing
2	2	1 - 3	standing
		Round II	
Period	*Resting*	*Wrestling*	*Position*
1	3	1 (up) - 2 (down)	referee's
2	2	1 (up) - 3 (down)	referee's
		Round III	
Period	*Resting*	*Wrestling*	*Position*
1	3	1 (down) - 2 (up)	referee's
2	2	1 (down) - 3 (up)	referee's

In the first period of round one the varsity wrestler competes with wrestler 2 for takedowns. In period two, while wrestler number 2 is resting, he competes for takedowns with wrestler 3.

Round two finds the varsity man on top the entire time, and in round three on the bottom the full time. He continually wrestles either 2 or 3 while the other rests.

This drill can be run for any repeated number of rounds.

#2—Three-On-One Rotational Drill

The first-string varsity wrestler in each weight class is paired with the second-, third-, and fourth-string men of approximately the same weight. The varsity wrestler stays on the mat continuously while the other three men rotate in against him.

The drill has three rounds of three periods to a round.

		Round I	
Period	*Resting*	*Wrestling*	*Position*
1	3 & 4	1 - 2	standing
2	2 & 4	1 - 3	standing
3	3 & 2	1 - 4	standing
		Round II	
Period	*Resting*	*Wrestling*	*Position*
1	3 & 4	1 (up) - 2 (down)	referee's
2	2 & 4	1 (up) - 3 (down)	referee's
3	3 & 2	1 (up) - 4 (down)	referee's
		Round III	
Period	*Resting*	*Wrestling*	*Position*
1	3 & 4	1 (down) - 2 (up)	referee's
2	2 & 4	1 (down) - 3 (up)	referee's
3	3 & 2	1 (down) - 4 (up)	referee's

In round one the varsity wrestler competes with the second-string man in the first period, the third-string man in the second period, and the fourth-string man in the third period. Whenever a takedown is consummated both wrestlers immediately resume the standing position and go at it again until time runs out.

Round two is conducted in the same manner as round one with the exception that the varsity man remains in the top position throughout all three periods. Anytime a reversal or escape occurs, wrestling is halted and the original referee's position is resumed. Wrestling is then continued on the third slap of the defensive man's hand on the mat.

Round three finds the varsity man on the bottom the entire time. Each of the other three men takes his turn on top.

#3—Three-Man Rotational Drill

The team is divided into groups of three with the wrestlers in each group being given the numbers 1, 2, and 3. It is important that the members of each group be as close to the same weight as possible.

The drill, as illustrated below, is composed of three rounds.

Round I

Period	Referee	Wrestling	Position
1	1	2 - 3	standing
2	2	1 (up) - 3 (down)	referee's
3	3	1 (down) - 2 (up)	referee's

Round II

Period	Referee	Wrestling	Position
1	1	2 (up) - 3 (down)	referee's
2	2	1 - 3	standing
3	3	1 (up) - 2 (down)	referee's

Round III

Period	Referee	Wrestling	Position
1	1	2 (down) - 3 (up)	referee's
2	2	1 (down) - 3 (up)	referee's
3	3	1 - 2	standing

Round one has three periods. Wrestler number 1 acts as the official during the first period. He enforces the rules and keeps the score while numbers 2 and 3 wrestle from the neutral standing position. After each takedown the wrestlers resume the standing posture.

The second period of round one finds wrestler 2 in the role of the official. The other two wrestlers assume the referee's position with wrestler 1 on top and 3 on the bottom. Anytime a reversal or escape occurs, both men revert back to the referee's position and begin again.

In the third period wrestler 3 becomes the official. Wrestler 1 is on the bottom with number 2 on top. Both men wrestle until the period ends.

This same procedure is followed until three rounds, or a total of nine periods, have been wrestled.

#4—Four-Man Rotational Drill

The drill is organized by dividing the wrestlers into groups of four of approximately the same weight. In each group the wrestlers are assigned numbers 1 through 4.

Round I

Period	Wrestling	Wrestling	Position
1	1 - 2	3 - 4	standing
2	1 - 3	2 - 4	standing
3	1 - 4	2 - 3	standing

Round II

Period	Wrestling	Wrestling	Position
1	1 (up) - 2 (down)	3 (up) - 4 (down)	referee's
2	1 (up) - 3 (down)	2 (up) - 4 (down)	referee's
3	1 (up) - 4 (down)	2 (up) - 3 (down)	referee's

Round III

Period	Wrestling	Wrestling	Position
1	1 (down) - 2 (up)	3 (down) - 4 (up)	referee's
2	1 (down) - 3 (up)	2 (down) - 4 (up)	referee's
3	1 (down) - 4 (up)	2 (down) - 3 (up)	referee's

To start, wrestler number 1 wrestles 2, and 3 wrestles 4 for take-downs. Period two of round one has 1 versus 3, and 2 versus 4. The final period of round one has 1 wrestling 4, and 2 wrestling 3.

In rounds two and three the wrestlers are competing on the mat. The same rotational procedure is used in both these rounds. Each wrestler is thereby given an opportunity to wrestle in both the top and bottom positions.

#5—Six-Man Rotational Drill

Six wrestlers are used in this drill. Two of the six—usually first-string men stay out on the mat continuously. Each competes in a separate bout simultaneously with the other.

To clarify how the drill is organized and conducted, the first two periods of round one are described in detail below.

Round I

Period	Resting	Wrestling	Wrestling	Position
1	4 & 6	1 - 5	2 - 3	standing
2	3 & 5	1 - 6	2 - 4	standing
3	3 & 6	1 - 4	2 - 5	standing
4	4 & 5	1 - 3	2 - 6	standing

Round II

Period	Resting	Wrestling	Wrestling	Position
1	4 & 6	1 (up) - 5 (down)	2 (up) - 3 (down)	referee's
2	3 & 5	1 (up) - 6 (down)	2 (up) - 4 (down)	referee's
3	3 & 6	1 (up) - 4 (down)	2 (up) - 5 (down)	referee's
4	4 & 5	1 (up) - 3 (down)	2 (up) - 6 (down)	referee's

Round III

Period	Resting	Wrestling	Wrestling	Position
1	4 & 6	1 (down) - 5 (up)	2 (down) - 3 (up)	referee's
2	3 & 5	1 (down) - 6 (up)	2 (down) - 4 (up)	referee's
3	3 & 6	1 (down) - 4 (up)	2 (down) - 5 (up)	referee's
4	4 & 5	1 (down) - 3 (up)	2 (down) - 6 (up)	referee's

Periods one and two of round one are wrestled in a neutral standing position. In period one of round one, wrestlers 4 and 6 rest while 5 wrestles 1, and 3 wrestles 2. At the expiration of the first period, wrestler 3 assumes the rest position formerly occupied by wrestler 4 and wrestler 5 assumes the rest position occupied by wrestler 6. Wrestler 4 moves up to wrestle 2 while wrestler 6 wrestles 1. In all three rounds numbers 1 and 2 are wrestling continuously. This rotation is continued until three rounds of four periods each are completed. Rounds two and three are conducted from the referee's position.

#6—Sixteen-Man Rotational Drill

In this drill eight circles are used. Each circle is approximately eleven feet in diameter and equally separated from the other circles. The eight circles are divided into two groups.

The lighter wrestlers are placed in one of the two groups of circles while the heavier wrestlers are placed in the other. Those wrestlers of approximately the same weight are then paired up and placed in the circles in the referee's position. In each of the two groups of circles the wrestlers are then given the numbers 1 through 8. The wrestlers in each circle will wrestle a predetermined period of time before rotating.

Period I

Circle	Circle	Wrestling	Position
126	155	1 (up) - 2 (down)	referee's
132	167	3 (up) - 4 (down)	referee's
138	185	5 (up) - 6 (down)	referee's
145	Hwt	7 (up) - 8 (down)	referee's

Period II

Circle	Circle	Wrestling	Position
126	155	8 (up) - 2 (down)	referee's
132	167	3 (up) - 1 (down)	referee's
138	185	4 (up) - 6 (down)	referee's
145	Hwt	7 (up) - 5 (down)	referee's

Period III

Circle	Circle	Wrestling	Position
126	155	5 (up) - 2 (down)	referee's
132	167	3 (up) - 8 (down)	referee's
138	185	1 (up) - 6 (down)	referee's
145	Hwt.	7 (up) - 4 (down)	referee's

Period IV

Circle	Circle	Wrestling	Position
126	155	4 (up) - 2 (down)	referee's
132	167	3 (up) - 5 (down)	referee's
138	185	8 (up) - 6 (down)	referee's
145	Hwt	7 (up) - 1 (down)	referee's

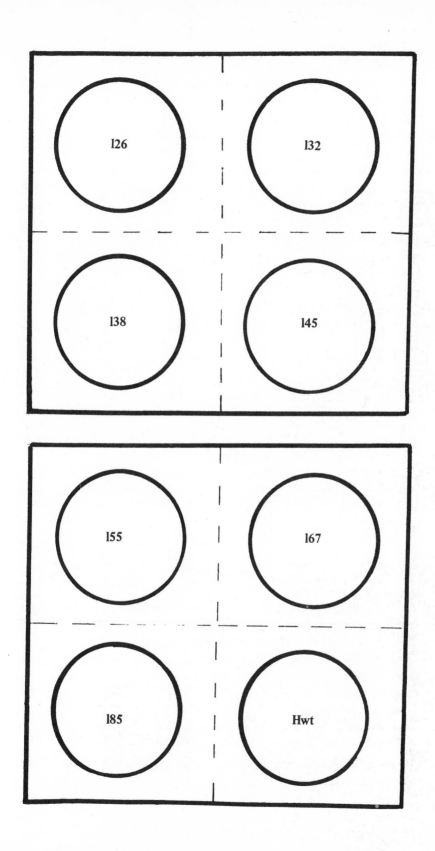

Then, on the signal, the wrestler in the top position in the 126 circle moves into the bottom position of the 132 circle. The wrestler who occupied the bottom position in the 132 circle moves to the top position in the 138 circle. The man in the top position here in the 138 circle moves into the bottom position of the 145 circle. The wrestler who occupied the bottom position of the 145 circle moves to the 126 circle where he assumes the top position. This rotational sequence is followed at the end of each time period until the original formation is resumed. The sequence of rotation in the other group of four circles is the same as the one outlined above.

The fifth period begins with the wrestlers in their original circles.

Period V

Circle	Circle	Wrestling	Position
126	155	1 (up) - 2 (down)	referee's
132	167	3 (up) - 4 (down)	referee's
138	185	5 (up) - 6 (down)	referee's
145	Hwt	7 (up) - 8 (down)	referee's

Period VI

Circle	Circle	Wrestling	Position
126	155	1 (up) - 7 (down)	referee's
132	167	2 (up) - 4 (down)	referee's
138	185	5 (up) - 3 (down)	referee's
145	Hwt	6 (up) - 8 (down)	referee's

Period VII

Circle	Circle	Wrestling	Position
126	155	1 (up) - 6 (down)	referee's
132	167	7 (up) - 4 (down)	referee's
138	185	5 (up) - 2 (down)	referee's
145	Hwt	3 (up) - 8 (down)	referee's

Period VIII

Circle	Circle	Wrestling	Position
126	155	1 (up) - 3 (down)	referee's
132	167	6 (up) - 4 (down)	referee's
138	185	5 (up) - 7 (down)	referee's
145	Hwt	2 (up) - 8 (down)	referee's

This time, at the end of the fifth period, the bottom man from the 126 circle moves to the top position of the 132 circle. The top man in the 132 circle moves to the bottom position of the 138 circle. The wrestler occupying the bottom position in the 138 circle moves up to the 145 circle and replaces the top man. The top man in the 145 circle moves to the bottom position in the 126 circle. The cycle is repeated until eight periods of wrestling have been completed.

This drill allows each wrestler to move around from one weight to another while periodically assuming a different position.

Those wrestlers needing to work on breakdowns, rides, and hold-downs should be assigned odd numbers, while those who need to practice escapes and reversals should be given even numbers.

#7—Sixteen-Man Rotational Drill

The same eight circles as described in drill number 6 are used in this drill. The basic difference between the two drills is in the manner of rotation. In this drill it is only the bottom man that moves.

At the end of the first period, the 126 wrestler moves to the 132 circle. The wrestler he replaces moves to the 138 circle. The bottom wrestler occupying the 138 circle moves to the 145 circle. The 145 wrestler takes the place of the bottom wrestler in the 126 circle. This sequence concludes after four periods. It is outlined below:

		Period I	
Circle	*Circle*	*Wrestling*	*Position*
126	155	1 (up) - 2 (down)	referee's
132	167	3 (up) - 4 (down)	referee's
138	185	5 (up) - 6 (down)	referee's
145	Hwt	7 (up) - 8 (down)	referee's
		Period II	
Circle	*Circle*	*Wrestling*	*Position*
126	155	1 (up) - 8 (down)	referee's
132	167	3 (up) - 2 (down)	referee's
138	185	5 (up) - 4 (down)	referee's
145	Hwt	7 (up) - 6 (down)	referee's
		Period III	
Circle	*Circle*	*Wrestling*	*Position*
126	155	1 (up) - 6 (down)	referee's
132	167	3 (up) - 8 (down)	referee's
138	185	5 (up) - 2 (down)	referee's
145	Hwt	7 (up) - 4 (down)	referee's
		Period IV	
Circle	*Circle*	*Wrestling*	*Position*
126	155	1 (up) - 4 (down)	referee's
132	167	3 (up) - 6 (down)	referee's
138	185	5 (up) - 8 (down)	referee's
145	Hwt	7 (up) - 2 (down)	referee's

A slight variation in the continuation of this sequence is to have only the top men move after each period. The procedure is the same except that the bottom men remain stationary instead of the top men. The top men move through all four circles before the cycle is completed.

Period V

Circle	Circle	Wrestling	Position
126	155	1 (up) - 2 (down)	referee's
132	167	3 (up) - 4 (down)	referee's
138	185	5 (up) - 6 (down)	referee's
145	Hwt	7 (up) - 8 (down)	referee's

Period VI

Circle	Circle	Wrestling	Position
126	155	7 (up) - 2 (down)	referee's
132	167	1 (up) - 4 (down)	referee's
138	185	3 (up) - 6 (down)	referee's
145	Hwt	5 (up) - 8 (down)	referee's

Period VII

Circle	Circle	Wrestling	Position
126	155	5 (up) - 2 (down)	referee's
132	167	7 (up) - 4 (down)	referee's
138	185	1 (up) - 6 (down)	referee's
145	Hwt	3 (up) - 8 (down)	referee's

Period VIII

Circle	Circle	Wrestling	Position
126	155	3 (up) - 2 (down)	referee's
132	167	5 (up) - 4 (down)	referee's
138	185	7 (up) - 6 (down)	referee's
145	Hwt	1 (up) - 8 (down)	referee's

#8—Sixteen-Man Rotational Drill

The identical arrangement of eight circles used in drill number 6 are employed here. This drill varies from the previous two inasmuch as the wrestlers in each circle change positions with one another before either wrestler moves up to a different circle.

Specifically, at the end of each odd-numbered period, i.e., 1,3,5, 7, the wrestlers in each circle change around in the referee's position. After each even numbered period, i.e., 2, 4, 6, 8, the top man in the referee's position moves on to the next circle. This is outlined below:

Period I

Circle	Circle	Wrestling	Position
126	155	1 (up) - 2 (down)	referee's
132	167	3 (up) - 4 (down)	referee's
138	185	5 (up) - 6 (down)	referee's
145	Hwt	7 (up) - 8 (down)	referee's

Period II

Circle	Circle	Wrestling	Position
126	155	2 (up) - 1 (down)	referee's
132	167	4 (up) - 3 (down)	referee's
138	185	6 (up) - 5 (down)	referee's
145	Hwt	8 (up) - 7 (down)	referee's

Period III

Circle	Circle	Wrestling	Position
126	155	1 (up) - 8 (down)	referee's
132	167	3 (up) - 2 (down)	referee's
138	185	5 (up) - 4 (down)	referee's
145	Hwt	7 (up) - 6 (down)	referee's

Period IV

Circle	Circle	Wrestling	Position
126	155	8 (up) - 1 (down)	referee's
132	167	2 (up) - 3 (down)	referee's
138	185	4 (up) - 5 (down)	referee's
145	Hwt	6 (up) - 7 (down)	referee's

Period V

Circle	Circle	Wrestling	Position
126	155	1 (up) - 6 (down)	referee's
132	167	3 (up) - 8 (down)	referee's
138	185	5 (up) - 2 (down)	referee's
145	Hwt	7 (up) - 4 (down)	referee's

Period VI

Circle	Circle	Wrestling	Position
126	155	6 (up) - 1 (down)	referee's
Circle	167	8 (up) - 3 (down)	referee's
132	185	2 (up) - 5 (down)	referee's
138	Hwt	4 (up) - 7 (down)	referee's
145			

Period VII

Circle	Circle	Wrestling	Position
126	155	1 (up) - 4 (down)	referee's
132	167	3 (up) - 6 (down)	referee's
138	185	5 (up) - 8 (down)	referee's
145	Hwt	7 (up) - 2 (down)	referee's

Period VIII

Circle	Circle	Wrestling	Position
126	155	4 (up) - 1 (down)	referee's
132	167	6 (up) - 3 (down)	referee's
138	185	8 (up) - 5 (down)	referee's
145	Hwt	2 (up) - 7 (down)	referee's

#9—Twenty-Seven-Man Rotational Drill

Nine circles are evenly divided into three horizontal rows. Each horizontal row constitutes what is known as a circuit.

Three wrestlers of approximately the same weight are assigned to each circle and given numbers from one to three. The drill is then conducted according to the procedure outlined on the accompanying chart.

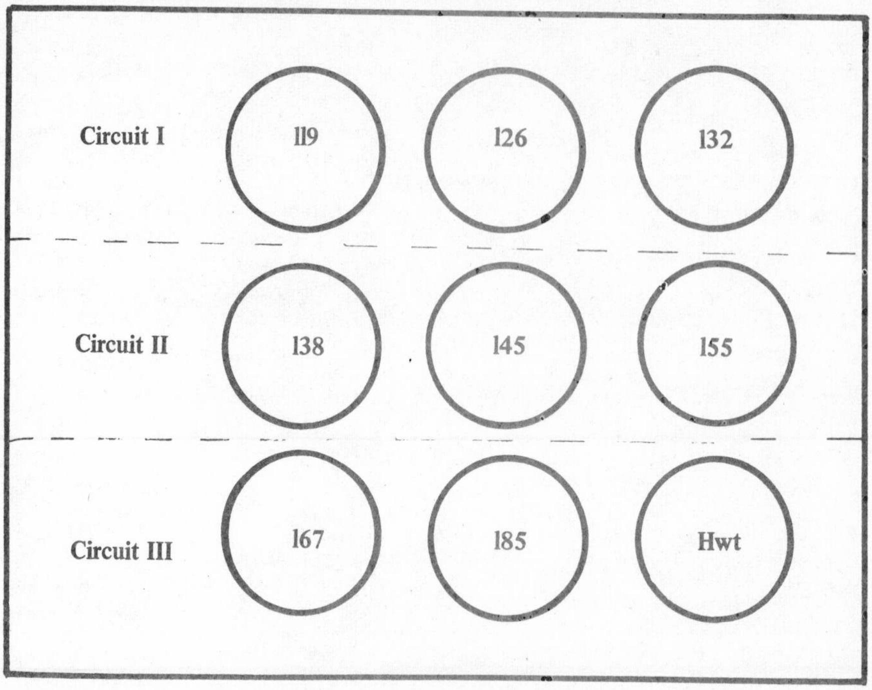

Circuit I	119	126	132
Circuit II	138	145	155
Circuit III	167	185	Hwt

Round I

Period	Resting	Wrestling	Position
1	1	2 - 3	standing
2	2	1 (up) - 3 (down)	referee's
3	3	1 (down) - 2 (up)	referee's

Round II

Period	Resting	Wrestling	Position
1	1	2 (up) - 3 (down)	referee's
2	2	1 - 3	standing
3	3	1 (up) - 2 (down)	referee's

Round III

Period	Resting	Wrestler	Position
1	1	2 (down) -3 (up)	referee's
2	2	1 (down) - 3 (up)	referee's
3	3	1 - 2	standing

In the first period of Round I wrestler number 1 rests while 2 and 3 wrestle from the standing position. After each takedown, they resume the standing position and try for another takedown.

In the second period of Round I, 2 rests while 1 and 3 wrestle from the referee's position with 1 on top. If 3 reverses or escapes, they quickly resume the original position and begin to wrestle again when the bottom man slaps the mat.

In the third period of Round I, 3 rests while 2 (on top) and 1 (on bottom) wrestle from the referee's position.

This same routine continues through the next two rounds (see chart) for a total of nine periods. At the end of the first three-round series, a whistle or vocal command tells the number 1 men to move up one circle within their horizontal rows. Number 1 in the 118 circle moves up to the 126 circle; number 1 at the 126 circle moves up to 132; and the number 1 man at 132 moves to the 119 circle. The same rotation is followed in the other two circuits.

To facilitate the rotation, clear-cut instructions for the direction of rotation must be given in advance. After the first few times, the pattern will be thoroughly understood and should run smoothly.

After the second series of three rounds, the number 2 men rotate in the same fashion as the number 1 men did previously. This completes the drill. Each boy will have wrestled eighteen complete three-period matches, ten in his own weight class, against six different opponents. He will have wrestled eighteen periods standing, eighteen periods in the top position, and eighteen periods in the down position. He will have wrestled two-thirds of the total time of the drill and rested one-third.

#10—Rotational Line Drill

The team is separated into four general weight ranges. There should not be a great weight variance between members of each group. One half of the wrestlers in each group are placed on the bottom in the referee's position.

During the drill the bottom men try to escape or reverse positions while the top men attempt to break the bottom men down and secure pinning combinations. After a predetermined interval of time the top men move down the row to the next wrestler in line. The last wrestler on top in each row moves up to the first man in the same row. This same procedure is followed until every top man has wrestled every bottom man in his row once.

The top and bottom men then switch positions and wrestling continues as before.

As a variation, either or both the top and/or the bottom men may be restricted to a limited number of moves that they are allowed to attempt.

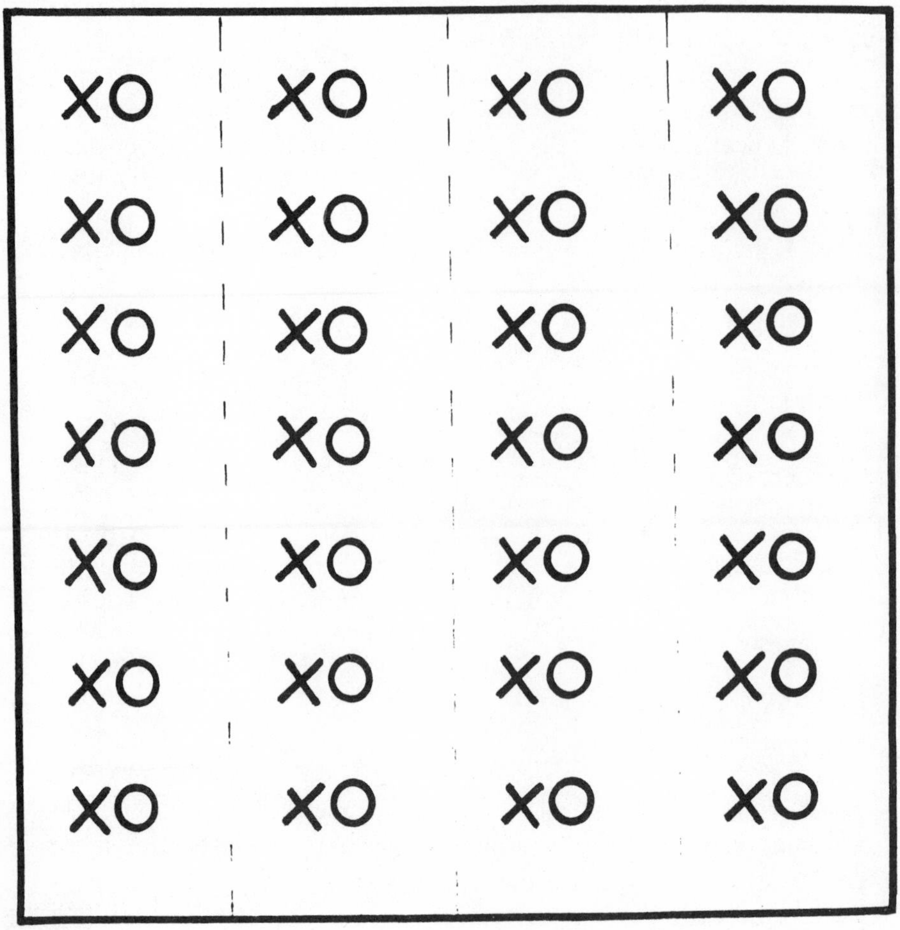

XO XO XO XO
XO XO XO XO
XO XO XO XO
XO XO XO XO
XO XO XO XO
XO XO XO XO
XO XO XO XO

#11—Rotational Perimeter Drill

The perimeter of the mat is used for this drill. The wrestlers are paired up and started in the referee's position facing in toward the center of the mat.

The bottom men attempt to escape or reverse while the top men work to break them down. After the predetermined period of time has elapsed one of the following procedures can be followed:

1. The top men move around the circle in a clockwise direction until all stationary men are wrestled.
2. The bottom men move around the circle in a clockwise direction until all stationary men are wrestled.
3. The top men move and assume the bottom position.
4. The bottom men move and assume the top position.

When a heavier man is paired with a much lighter partner, the heavier man must be conscious of his greater weight and strength so as to minimize the chances of causing injury. The lighter man must rely on his speed and try to outmaneuver his larger and stronger partner in order to be a challenge.

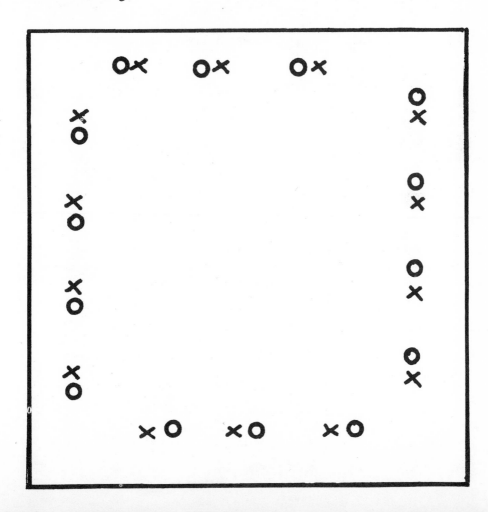

#12—Rotational Varsity Drill

The squad is divided into two equal-sized groups. One of the groups is made up of the heavier wrestlers while the other group is the lighter wrestlers.

Three of the first string varsity wrestlers from each group take on the rest of the men in each of their respective groups one at a time. The drill is then repeated with three other wrestlers from each group. The drill is completed when every wrestler has taken on the remainder of his group.

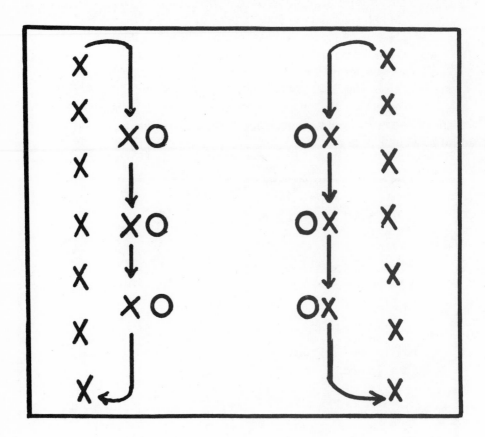

#13—Rotational Quarter Drill

The squad is divided into four groups. Each group is comprised of wrestlers of approximately the same weight. Each group occupies a quarter of the wrestling area.

The two groups with the heavier wrestlers assume a location on the same side of the mat. Then two wrestlers from each of the groups come onto the mat and wrestle each other.

At the end of the allotted time the wrestlers move according to the diagram below. Each wrestler has the opportunity to wrestle twice before going to the back of his respective line.

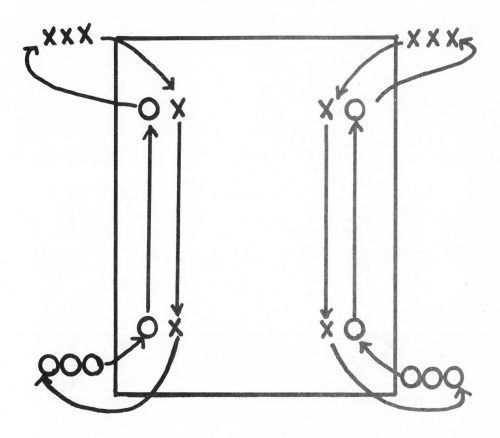

#14—Rotational Four-Corner Drill

Two pairs of wrestlers are placed at each of the four corners of the mat. They are instructed to either wrestle from standing or the referee's position. If wrestling from the referee's position, the wrestlers should be instructed to reverse positions before one of them rotates counterclockwise around the mat. This rotation is diagramed below.

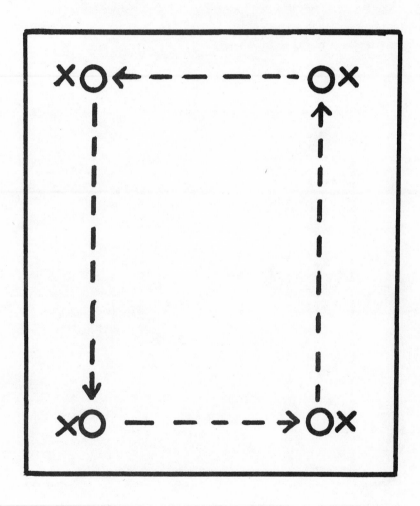

5
COMPETITIONAL DRILLS

The essence of any wrestling program is competition. Competition should be inserted into the program as often as possible. Considerably more can be accomplished, especially in terms of conditioning, when it is introduced into routine workouts.

Competition carries its own incentive. It:

1. Makes practicing skills more enjoyable and exciting.
2. Delays the onset of conscious fatigue.
3. Enhances interest.
4. Reduces the chances of boredom.
5. Encourages greater effort.

Boys participate in wrestling for the sake of competition. They want challenging opportunities to test themselves. Competition provides these opportunities. It is a means of measuring one's physical skills against a rival's.

The following drills have been divided into four broad areas of wrestling: takedown, top-man, bottom-man, and pinning drills.

COMPETITIVE TAKEDOWN DRILL

#15—Jump-Back Drill

The two wrestlers stand facing each other about a foot apart. The defensive wrestler has his eyes closed. The offensive man, whenever ready, drops down for the other wrestler's legs. The defensive wrestler jumps back as soon as he feels the contact.

Jumping back as contact is made.

#16—Handicap Drill

This drill is for the purpose of developing speed in countering take-downs. It begins with two wrestlers circling from an open stance. One wrestler has his hands clasped behind his back. The other man, the attacker, must not touch the defender except in a takedown attempt. The defender may then unclasp his hands and attempt to counter the attack.

Beginning with the hands clasped behind the back.

#17—Five-Point Drill

This drill places special emphasis on going directly into a pinning situation from a takedown. Its purpose is to develop within the boy an alertness to capitalize upon pinning possibilities immediately following takedowns. Only takedowns accompanied by near falls or falls are counted in this drill.

Taking the opponent down.

Going directly into a pinning situation.

#18—Twice-Around Drill

The squad is divided into four groups by weight. The most skilled boy from each group is placed on the mat while the other wrestlers line up ready to compete against him.

He must go through the line twice in succession before sitting down. In other words, he must take on each of the other wrestlers twice before he gets to rest.

The next-best boy of the remaining wrestlers then takes on the remaining boys in succession twice. This procedure continues until only two boys remain. They must wrestle each other for two takedowns.

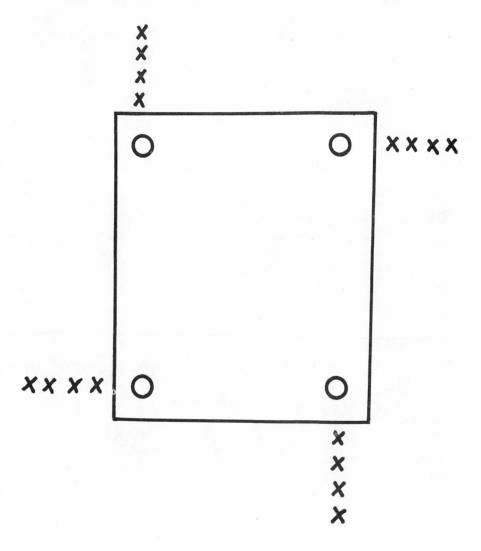

#19—Two-Man Drill

The wrestlers are paired off and given thirty seconds to execute a successful takedown. If a takedown is gained, wrestling continues until they hear the whistle. If the boy taken down escapes or reverses before the time limit expires, the takedown is not counted. A variation of this procedure would be to have both boys begin standing again after each takedown.

Other ways of varying the drill include requiring all takedowns to be:

1. Initiated from an open stance.
2. Initiated from a tie-up position.
3. Initiated from a stance where one or both of the wrestlers are down on one knee.
4. Initiated with only one particular takedown being attempted such as:
   a. Duck under.
   b. Single leg.
   c. Double leg.
   d. Arm drag.

Beginning in a tie-up position.

#20—Group Drill

All wrestlers form a line along one side of the mat with the heaviest boys at one end and the lightest boys at the other end.

The two lightest wrestlers come out to the center and begin the drill by working for a takedown within a thirty-second time limit. If no takedown occurs the next two wrestlers in line replace the first two. If, however, one boy succeeds in taking the other to the mat, he is challenged by the next wrestler in line closest to his weight. He will continue to wrestle until taken down.

A slight variation is to have the initial starters wrestle until one wrestler secures two takedowns. If no takedown is obtained in one minute both wrestlers rejoin the line.

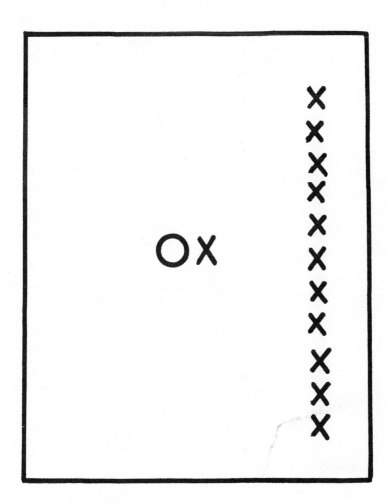

#21—King-of-the-Mat Drill

In this drill a total of four groups are formed. Members of each group are approximately the same weight. Each group is assigned a portion of the mat area.

Two boys from each group come out and go for a takedown. The boy who gets the takedown within a specified period of time (usually twenty to thirty seconds) is considered to be king of the mat. He continues to reign as king until a challenger from his group takes him down and, thereby, becomes the new king.

A variation of this drill is to have the first wrestler in each line, the king, wrestle every boy in his line twice for takedowns at twenty-second intervals. When he finishes, he goes to the end of the line and the next boy in line becomes the king. He also goes through the line twice. This continues until each wrestler has had a turn at being king.

A third variation is to have the loser stay out on the mat and the winner (the king) go to the end of the line. The loser is expected to wrestle until he wins. In this way, those wrestlers needing the most work on takedowns get it.

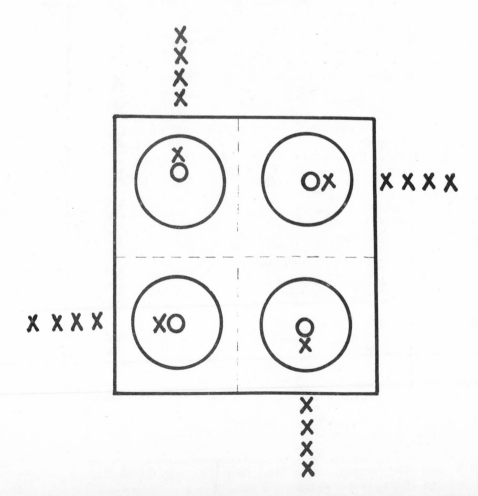

#22—Endless Relay Drill

The squad is divided into two teams of equal ability. The members of each team line up from lightest to heaviest, facing each other from opposite sides of the mat.

The two lightest wrestlers begin the competition. Then, according to the chart shown below, one of the two wrestlers stays out on the mat to compete with the next-heaviest wrestler from the other team.

TEAM I Wrestler		TEAM II Wrestler
A	vs.	W
A	vs.	X
B	vs.	X
B	vs.	Y
C	vs.	Y
C	vs.	Z
D	vs.	Z
D	vs.	Y
C	vs.	Y
C	vs.	X
B	vs.	X
B	vs.	W

Go back to start (A vs. W)

Each wrestler competes twice before being replaced by a teammate. Team scores are kept. Wrestling continues for as long as desired.

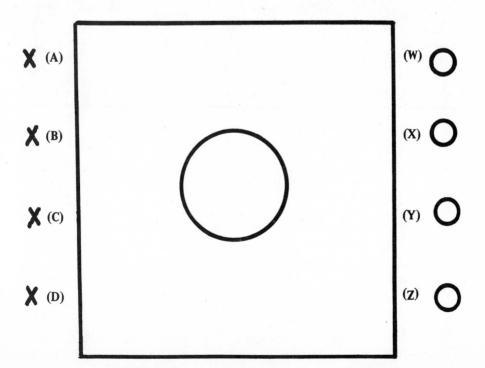

#23—Wrestle-Off Drill

To make the varsity team a boy should be expected to beat all the other challengers in his weight class. To eliminate unfair weight advantages the challenger should be expected to be no more than three pounds above their weight classification before being allowed to challenge.

Such challenge matches develop team morale by conveying the idea that there is always room at the top for a boy who can prove he should be there. The first string boy is kept from becoming complacent by having to prove he is the best.

Challenging the first-string varsity wrestlers.

COMPETITIVE TOP-MAN DRILLS

#24—Hand-Reaction Drill

The wrestlers are paired off in the referee's position. The coach then announces the breakdown he expects the top man to attempt, i.e., cross-face and far ankle, far arm and near ankle, near arm and tight waist, etc. On the whistle the top man moves only his hands to the positions necessary to execute the breakdown.

On the next command, "Ready," he returns his hands to the original referee's position.

On the second whistle he executes the complete breakdown.

On the command "Ready" both wrestlers resume the referee's position.

On the third whistle the top man attempts the complete breakdown while the bottom man resists by attempting any escape or reversal he chooses.

On the command "Ready" the wrestlers change places and assume the referee's position.

The drill is then repeated as often as desired.

Reaching for the far ankle and far arm.

#25—Breakdown Drill

The top man attempts to break the bottom man down to the mat by removing any of his points of support. The bottom man does nothing but attempt to maintain his all-fours position.

Removing a supporting limb.

#26—Counter Drill

The top man blocks and counters all escapes and reversals attempted by the bottom man. After each block or counter, he permits the bottom man to return to an all-fours position. No holddowns are employed. He is expected to maintain a floating position.

The bottom man uses any or all the methods he knows to escape. If he succeeds in getting away or gaining the position of advantage, both wrestlers stop and return to the referee's position to begin again.

After a reasonable period of time, the coach has both wrestlers switch positions.

A variation of this drill is to have the top man switch to the opposite side when beginning in the referee's position.

Countering the sit out.

#27—*Restricted Ride Drill*

The wrestlers are paired off by weight. The wrestler on top attempts to maintain control of the bottom man by using only one riding technique, i.e., cross body, navy, two on one, tight waist, etc. He must follow the bottom man who is attempting to escape or reverse. After the top man has worked to maintain the same ride a predetermined number of times, the positions are reversed and the drill is continued.

The drill exposes the top man to all the defensive tricks the bottom man knows to counter any particular ride.

Employing a cross-body ride.

#28—Maintain Control Drill

The wrestlers are paired off. The coach designates which two rides he wants the top man to employ. The top man puts one of the rides on before the whistle is blown. The top man must then change to the second ride without losing control while the bottom man attempts to counter.

After the top man has worked from one ride to the second a few times the wrestlers change positions.

Maintaining control.

#29—Ride Release Drill

The wrestlers are paired up in the referee's position. Before the signal is given to begin the wrestler on top applies the particular ride suggested by the coach.

The object of the drill is for the top man to attempt to maintain his position of advantage, but never to allow the bottom man to reverse him. He is expected to release the ride before he gets into serious trouble. He must attempt to maintain control only up to the point where he can avoid being reversed. He must be prepared to permit the bottom man to escape if necessary.

Being prepared, if necessary, to release the opponent.

COMPETIVE BOTTOM-MAN DRILLS

#30—Maintain Base Drill

The bottom man attempts to maintain his base while the top man works to break him down to the mat. The bottom man makes no attempt to escape or reverse, but simply fights to keep his all-fours position.

Working to keep an all-fours position.

#31—Two-Move Drill

In this drill the bottom man is limited to two moves. He must repeatedly attempt these same two moves time after time. This forces him to be exposed to all the counters the top man knows for these two moves.

Sitting out and turning in.

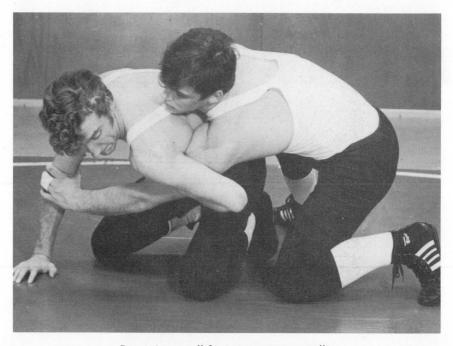

Returning to all fours to attempt a roll.

#32—Reversal Drill

Special emphasis is placed on reversing the top man. Escapes mean nothing and may even be counted against the bottom man. Only reversals are recognized. Once the bottom man gains the position of advantage he attempts to remain on top until the end of the time limit.

Reversing the top man.

#33—Explosive Stand-Up Drill

The wrestlers are paired off into two lines at one end of the mat. Both lines are facing in the same direction in an all-fours position.

On the whistle the wrestlers in both lines sprint out. The objective of each man in the second line is to tackle the man in front before he gets to the other end of the mat.

This drill develops the incentive to explode into a standing escape and keep moving.

A variation is to have the wrestlers line up and sprint out by individual weight classes.

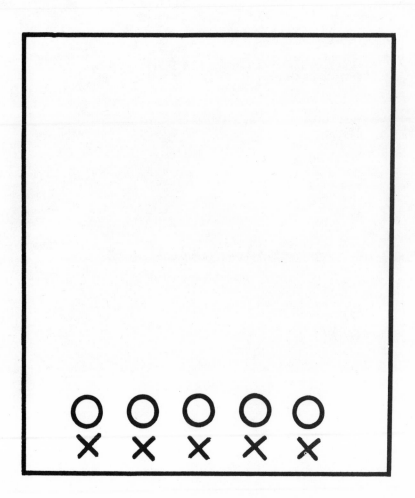

COMPETITIVE PINNING DRILLS

#34—Escape-a-Pin Drill

In this drill one man lies flat on his back and permits the other wrestler to apply any pinning combination of his choice. On the whistle the bottom man attempts to escape from the pinning hold by turning onto his stomach.

A variation of this drill is to have the start of the pinning combination applied to the bottom man while he is in a prone position or lying on one side. The bottom man then attempts to prevent the top man from turning him onto his back and pinning him.

Bridging to escape a pin.

6
SITUATIONAL DRILLS

Situational drills emphasize learning how to effectively handle specific circumstances that commonly arise in competition. By placing a wrestler in varied problematic situations that present a variety of alternatives, he is forced to evaluate and choose those moves which he thinks are most likely to succeed. He must take into account such things as the score, the period, the time remaining, and his relative position on the mat.

Almost any combination of match conditions can be simulated. Situations can be created that range from commonplace to unique.

The wrestler learns to (1) anticipate situations instantly,, (2) think analytically, and (3) time holds properly. The experience he gains in recognizing and successfully coping with these situations will give him a winning edge in competition.

Each of the drills in this chapter lasts from fifteen to thirty seconds. The number of drills that can be created, in addition to those presented here, is limited only by the coach's imagination. Coaches are encouraged to make up others to fit particular favored circumstances.

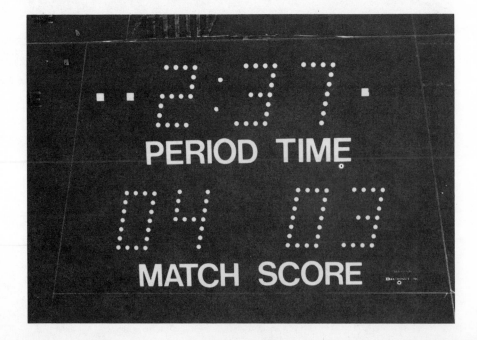

#35—Reaction Standing Drills

To begin, the wrestlers are paired up, standing and facing one another. One of the two men is put in the position of being halfway through a particular takedown. His partner is placed in a position of countering that takedown. Both men are instructed to do their best.

Standing Reaction Situations:
1. A single leg attempt is being countered by a standing whizzer.
2. A double leg attempt is being countered by a sprawl.
3. A double leg attempt is being countered by a sprawl and crossface.
4. A fireman's carry is being countered by a underhook (cow catcher).
5. An arm drag is in the process of being completed to a go behind.

Reacting to a counter for the single-leg takedown.

#36—Reaction Top-Man Drills

Members of the team are paired up. The pairs of wrestlers are then placed into particular situations and told to do their best to gain or maintain the position of advantage.

Top-Man Reaction Situations:
A. The top man must react to the bottom man's being halfway through a:
    1. Sit out.
    2. Side roll.
    3. Switch.
    4. Stand up.
    5. Whizzer.
B. The top man must:
    1. Turn the bottom man, who is prone, over into a pinning combination.
    2. Change from one pinning combination to another without allowing the bottom man to escape.
    3. Break the bottom man down while the bottom man attempts to maintain a stable position on his hands and knees.

Reacting to a stand up.

#37—Reaction Bottom-Man Drills

The wrestlers are paired off. Each pair is told to start from one of the positions described below.

Bottom-Man Reaction Situations:
The bottom man must react to the top man's:
1. Cross-body ride.
2. Tight-waist ride.
3. Far-ankle and tight-waist ride.
4. Navy ride.
5. Near-arm and far-ankle ride.

Reacting to a navy ride.

#38—Standing Situation Drills

These drills involve situations where both wrestlers, A and B, are standing. Each drill is either fifteen or thirty seconds in duration.

A. fifteen-second standing drills.
1. A is losing by one point late in the match and must get a takedown to win.
2. A can only win by a pin. He must go from a takedown into a pinning combination.
3. A is leading 4–3 with both wrestlers on their feet in a neutral standing position.
4. The score is tied with A having just gone behind B in a rear standing position. A has both hands locked around B's waist and must take him to the mat to earn a takedown.

B. Thirty-second standing drills:
1. The score is tied 2–2 in the second overtime period.
2. B is leading by one point late in the match. He must block or counter takedown attempts to win.
3. B is leading by one point, but has been warned for stalling.

Standing tied-up position.

#39—Top-Man Situation Drills

In these drills, wrestler A is put into situations that involve late-match scoring urgency. In most instances he must either initiate an effective attack to win or avert a loss by rebuffing the opponent's attempts to score.

Fifteen- to thirty-second top-man drills.
1. A is trailing by one point in overtime.
2. The score is tied. A is on top and can win if he can ride out the period.
3. A is leading 5–3 while on top in the referee's position.
4. A is leading by one point, but has been warned for stalling.
5. A is two points ahead. He can allow an escape for one point, but can't afford to have his opponent gain a reversal.

Starting bottom man's position.

#40—Bottom-Man Situation Drills

Wrestler B is on the bottom late in the match. In each of the following situations the score is close or tied and time is running out.

Fifteen- to thirty-second bottom-man drills:

1. B is one point behind and must score a reversal to win.
2. B is winning by a substantial margin. He can only lose if he is turned over and pinned.
3. B has a slight lead in the score, but cannot be scored upon if he hopes to win.
4. In overtime B is leading by one point and is being ridden with a crossbody ride.
5. B is behind by one point. He has stood up, but A still controls one of his legs.

Starting top man's position.

7
EDUCATIONAL DRILLS

Educational-type drills are an absolute necessity if a team of championship caliber is to be developed.

When preparing to present these type of drills, the following principles should be taken into account:

1. Every wrestling maneuver can be broken down into its component parts. Repetitive practice of each part results in a more complete learning experience. It is only after each part is skillfully learned that the entire maneuver can be performed effectively.
2. Every maneuver is composed of certain moves that are deemed of vital importance. By extracting these specifics from the particular maneuver being learned they can be incorporated into an educational drill. The wrestler's efforts are thereby focused on building proficiency in the important parts of the maneuver.
3. Every maneuver is composed of simple and complex aspects. Drills should be programmed from the simple elements to the complex with the intention of having them repeated often enough to reach the subconscious level.

#41—Passive-Resistance Drill

The wrestlers are paired off. One of each pair is designated as being the offensive man. He executes setups, takedowns, go behinds, rides, breakdowns, holddowns, pins, escapes, reversals, and counters as directed by the coach. The defensive wrestler offers only token resistance. He is not completely submissive, but rather sufficiently resistant to require the move be correctly applied for it to work. He makes no attempt to counter the move.

After a reasonable period of time the positions of the two wrestlers are reversed.

Offering passive resistance.

#42—Mixed Drill

In this drill the heavier wrestlers work with the lighter, quicker men. This combination requires the lighter wrestlers to explode into their moves rather than attempting to muscle heavier, stronger men.

Working with a heavier wrestler.

#43—Look-Away Drill

The wrestlers are paired off and placed in the referee's position. The coach instructs one of the wrestlers to look away while he indicates to the other wrestler the move or series of moves he wants him to attempt. A blackboard, printed cards, or hand signals (holding up one or two arms) can be used to identify the moves to be attempted. Wrestlers who are near-sighted should be located closer to the blackboard or coach.

On the signal both wrestlers go all-out for fifteen to thirty seconds. At the end of the allotted time the wrestlers reverse positions and the drill continues.

A variation of this drill is to have half of each pair of wrestlers come together into a huddle with the coach. Secret instructions are then given to each one as to what to attempt. The element of secrecy makes this drill an enjoyable game.

Looking away.

#44—Reward-Penalty Drill

In this drill the boy who fails to accomplish what the coach directs must pay a penalty. For example, the boy who fails to get the first takedown, to escape, to reverse, to pin, etc. can be required to do a specific number of laps, push-ups, or sit-ups.

The opposite of penalties is to give rewards. Examples of rewards are as follows:

1. Those who get away, get the first three takedowns, etc., are permitted to shower early.
2. Those who earn the first takedown get to rest. Those taken down must stay on the mat until they are successful.

A slight variation of this drill is to assign a penalty of fifty push-ups to every wrestler before starting. For each takedown gained the wrestler may subtract five push-ups from that total.

Paying the penalty.

#45—Numbers Drill

This drill begins with the coach demonstrating a new technique in its entirety. Next, he breaks the move down into its component parts. A sequential series of numbers is then assigned to each part.

When the first number is given, the wrestlers execute the first part of the technique. This is followed by the second, third, and so on numbers until the entire technique is completed.

The coach should move around among the wrestlers, checking to see that all phases of the move are being properly executed.

Executing the first phase of a reversal technique.

#46—Blindfold Drill

The wrestlers are paired off. Either one or both wrestlers are blind-folded. The blindfolds can be made by cutting two-inch strips from an old innertube. This type of blindfold does not require tying and will expand to fit most any size head.

The wrestlers can be started from standing or on the mat. If started from standing all takedowns must be initiated from a tie-up position.

Down on the mat, blindfolding helps to develop the ability to sense body position. The wrestler is unable to rely on his sight. He must depend on other senses such as touch and balance. These senses are sharpened as a means of compensating for his loss of sight.

Blindfolding as a means of sharpening the senses.

#47—Hand-Control Drill

The proper execution of most wrestling techniques requires that the hands be freed or the opponent's hands be controlled. Rarely, however, does this elementary phase of wrestling receive adequate attention. It is often taken for granted. Efficient hand control improves the chances of success.

This drill can be conducted from a neutral standing position, the referee's position, or with the opponent in a rear standing position. Wrestlers attempt to tie up the other's hands while keeping their own free.

The drill is timed with the wrestlers changing positions after a few trials.

Controlling the opponent's hand.

#48—Stopwatch Drill

The coach assigns a series of moves to pairs of wrestlers. He then uses a stopwatch to time each pair to ascertain the fastest time for completion of the series.

A variation of this drill is to check how long it takes a pair of wrestlers to repeat a particular technique a specific number of times, i.e., fifteen sit outs.

Repeating a single technique several times.

#49—Sprawl Drill

This drill has all the wrestlers facing in one direction while running in place. On the command "Sprawl," they drop to their stomachs while extending their legs backward.

A variation is to have pairs of wrestlers start by facing each other in a neutral standing position. On the coach's signal one wrestler drops down for the other's legs. The other wrestler responds by throwing his legs back, arching his back, and pressing his stomach toward the mat.

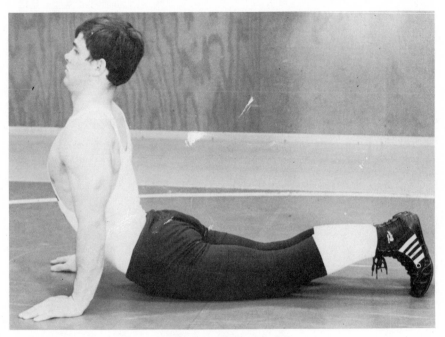

Sprawling on command.

#50—Leg-Takedown Drill

The drill begins with the team running in place. On the whistle the wrestlers are expected to drop and slide forward as if going for a double-leg takedown. As soon as their knees touch the mat they should return to their feet and continue running in place until the next whistle.

A variation of this drill starts with having the wrestlers line up along the wall. On the whistle they "shoot" in for a leg takedown trying to get their knees as close to the wall as possible. As the drill progresses, the distance from the wall is gradually increased.

A third variation is to have the wrestlers line up and slide forward as if shooting for a leg takedown by going under the coachs outstretched arm. If done properly, the wrestlers will slide forward on their knees as they pass under the arm. Emphasis should be on keeping their heads up, weight over their haunches, and their backs straight.

Sliding forward to a double-leg takedown position.

#51—Scarecrow Drill

Wrestlers line up in single file. The first man in the line turns and faces the other wrestlers. He then assumes a scarecrow position with his arms extended out to both sides. An object such as a knee pad, headgear, sponge, or folded towel is placed between his legs.

The next wrestler in line assumes a position approximately an arm's length in front of the scarecrowed wrestler. On the whistle he attempts to reach around and grab the object before the defensive man can pick it up.

The offensive man then assumes the scarecrow position and the next wrestler in line attempts the same thing. The defensive man goes to the end of the line.

Shooting in and grabbing.

#52—Repetition Drill

Members of the team are placed in an all-fours position on the mat. On the whistle they are to repeat one move continuously until the next whistle stops them. For example the wrestlers could be expected to repeat sit outs (turned in or out), switches, or rolls.

Repeating a technique.

#53—Quick Stand-Up Drill

The wrestlers line up in an all-fours position across one end of the mat. Each should be tense and ready to explode out to standing. On the whistle they stand up and sprint to the far end of the mat. The coach calls out the first- and second-place finishers.

A variation of this drill is simply to have the wrestlers stand up quickly, in place, on the whistle and return to an all-fours position on the command of "Ready."

Standing up quickly.

#54—Float Drill

The drill begins with one wrestler down on all fours and the other wrestler on top with his elbows clamped to the bottom man's sides.

The bottom man is permitted to do anything to dislodge the man on top by the speed of his movements. Twisting, crawling, sitting out, and making circular turns are techniques commonly employed. He may not, however, stand up or apply any grip or hold.

The top man cannot use his hands to hold on although he may use the inside of his arms to exert inward pressure to maintain a floating position. Almost all of his weight should be over the bottom man and very little supported by his legs. He must move with the bottom man while attempting to keep contact at all times.

Floating position.

#55—Move-Up Drill

From the referee's position the bottom man attempts to gain a standing posture, thereby removing the weight of the top man from his back.

He is allowed to attempt anything legal that will enable him to secure a standing posture. Emphasis should be on controlling the opponent's hands.

The task of the top man is to keep the bottom wrestler from gaining altitude.

Moving up while controlling the opponent's hands.

#56—Spin Drill

This drill begins with one wrestler in an all-fours position. His head is lowered. The top man places his chest, as a pivot point, on the bottom man's back. He spins around and around in quarter, half, and full turns. He spins as rapidly as possible, changing directions on the coach's command. He keeps his legs well back out of reach and uses them as seldom as possible for propelling his body around. He uses his hands to maintain balance, but never allows them to touch the mat.

A variation of this drill is to have the bottom man raise an arm to block the legs of the top man momentarily if he fails to keep them out of reach.

Another variation is to have the bottom man attempt to keep the top man in front of him. He may spin, move forward or backward, in accomplishing this objective. The top man tries to get behind the bottom man by spinning without the use of his arms.

Spinning position.

#57—Tight Waist-Ride Drill

The wrestlers begin in the referee's position. The top man applies a tight waist ride. On the whistle he must work to maintain his one-arm waist ride. The bottom man tries to scramble away—from the top man while remaining on his hands and knees. He may spin, buck, and move quickly to get away.

Riding with a tight waist.

#58—Dummy Drill

The wrestlers line up in front of a football tackling dummy. On the whistle the first man in line slides in for a double-leg takedown. Emphasis is on penetration and form. The drill continues until each man has attempted the movement X number of times.

Penetrating for a takedown.

#59—Defense Drill

The wrestlers are paired off. The coach calls out a move. Before signaling to have the move attempted he pauses to give the defending wrestler an opportunity to think over how he is going to counter it.

Then on the whistle the offensive man initiates the move at full speed. The defensive wrestler counters the move as efficiently as possible.

Countering a whizzer.

#60—Second-Effort Drill

This drills begins with the wrestlers paired off in the neutral standing position. On the coach's whistle one of the two wrestlers, the offensive man, goes in for a particular takedown. The defensive man blocks the move but makes no attempt to gain the position of advantage.

As both wrestlers back out to resume the neutral stance, the offensive man shoots a second time for the same takedown.

An opponent will often unconsciously relax as he backs out of a stalemate. This is the opportune time to reattack.

Making a second effort.

#61—Touch-and-Go Drill

The wrestlers are paired and assume a neutral standing position facing each other. One wrestler of each pair is designated as the offensive man. On the signal the offensive man touches the defensive man's shoulder to set him up for a single or double leg takedown.

A slight variation is to have the offensive man touch one or twice, then fake the touch and shoot. An opponent will often expect to be touched again. When he isn't, the element of surprise is enough to allow the attacker get to his legs and take him down.

Setting up the takedown.

#62—Confidence Drill

This drill is most useful after having scouted an upcoming opponent.

The second- and third-string wrestlers in each weight class are linked together to form one "big man." The first string boy practices against this big man all week. The big man uses only those techniques favored by the next scheduled opponent.

The first string wrestler is exposed to the techniques that he is most likely to encounter. He develops confidence in knowing he is prepared to win. He is likely to enter the match with a more positive attitude.

Alternating with two wrestlers.

8
SEQUENTIAL DRILLS

Sequential drills may be defined as the linkage of several moves, blocks, and/or counters into a uniform uninterrupted series. They are designed to instill an automatic response of going from one move directly into another.

Sound wrestling requires that moves be executed in a continuous manner in accordance with movements of the opponent. Secondary moves that utilize the opponent's weakened position resulting from his having blocked an initial move are essential to success.

Failing to immediately attempt a second move after having the first blocked provides the opponent with time to prepare to block or counter each move. If a large gap of time elapses between a wrestler's initial move and his subsequent moves, the opponent will likely have little difficulty blocking or countering each one individually. Consequently, the effectiveness of any pattern is destroyed.

Isolated techniques are rarely successful. Only by merging techniques into some sort of sequence can the most positive results be realized. Each move must be one of a series of moves.

The best method of teaching chain wrestling is to select a limited number of moves and organize them into drills.

Sequential drills should, in general, be confined totally to either mat wrestling or to standing wrestling, but not both together. In this way most of the variations and counters to particular moves can be employed as a unit.

The general procedure for conducting sequential drills is first to keep them simple. Two- to four-step combinations should be taught. Then as the wrestlers become more skilled in the sequence more moves can be added to the series.

Each drill should be performed without hesitation between moves. As soon as the entire sequence has been completed, the wrestlers should be expected to return to the referee's position to await the next command.

Sequential drills aid in the recognition and anticpation of situations where an opponent is vulnerable. This vulnerability occurs most frequently when the opponent is given little time to adjust to changing circumstances. Time lapses for contemplating moves are performed in a series. Learning to perform moves in a series is best achieved through sequential wrestling drills.

#63—Sit-Out Drill

Sequence:
1. A sits out long and turns in.
2. B follows.
3. A sits out short and turns out.
4. B counters with a suck back.

Sitting out and turning in.

#64—Roll Drill

Sequence:
1. A attempts an outside roll.
2. B executes a step over.
3. A executes an outside roll to the opposite side.
4. B rerolls.
5. A attempts an outside roll.
6. B hangs back to a half nelson pin.

Attempting an outside roll.

#65—Switch Drill

Sequence:
1. A attempts an outside switch.
2. B counters by crowding with his inside hip.
3. A switches to the outside after regaining his base.
4. B reswitches.
5. A attempts to reswitch.
6. B counters with a limp arm and steps over.

Attempting an outside switch.

#66—*Whizzer Drill*

Sequence:

1. A whizzers.
2. B limp arms the whizzer.
3. A rewhizzers and grasps his inside thigh to prevent the limp arm counter.
4. B reaches for A's far arm to whip him over.
5. A avoids the reach by pulling his arm back out of reach.
6. B catches A's far arm and applies a half nelson and double-bar arm pin.

Whizzering the top man.

#67—Double-Leg Drill

Sequence:
1. A drops in for a double-leg takedown.
2. B sprawls.
3. A drives forward.
4. B grasps A's chin and overhooks A's arm.
5. A continues to pull B in and backheels him to the mat.

Dropping in for a double-leg takedown.

#68—Single-Leg Drill

Sequence:
1. A drops in for a single leg.
2. B bends his knee, places all his weight over the captured leg, and whizzers A's arm.
3. A lifts the captured leg off the mat.
4. B puts the leg on the outside of A's hip.
5. A steps back to lift the leg.
6. B puts the leg between A's legs.
7. A steps back, cradles the leg, and drops B to the mat.

Dropping in for a single-leg takedown.

#69—Stand-up Drill

Sequence:
1. A executes an inside leg stand up.
2. B counters with a back trip.
3. A performs an outside leg stand up.
4. B counters with a tilt.
5. A executes a bump back stand up.
6. B counters with a forward trip.
7. A stands up and tears B's hands apart for an escape.

Executing an inside-leg stand up.

#70—Combination Drill

Sequence:
1. A executes a short sit out and turn in.
2. B follows.
3. A switches to the outside.
4. Be reswitches.
5. A performs a long sit out and turn out.
6. B follows.
7. A employs an outside roll.
8. B rerolls.
9. A whizzers.
10. B limp arms.

Executing a short sit out.

9
EXERCITATIONAL DRILLS

Wrestling is a sport requiring the athlete to be in top-notch physical condition. Knowing all the holds in the world won't do him a bit of good if he can't compete for the full time of a regulation match without experiencing undue fatigue. It is a sport where being in condition means being able to pour it on in the third period and, if necessary, come from behind to win. More matches are lost in the final minutes because of poor conditioning than for any other single reason.

Diligent coaches are continually searching for newer, more effective methods of conditioning. Most contemporary methods of training do not vary greatly from one sport to the next. Wrestling, however, is an exception.

Coaches skeptical of popular methods of training athletes tend to feel these methods may fail to develop the specific type of endurance needed for wrestling. They are often of the opinion that the best training for wrestling is wrestling itself. However, they fail to recognize the fact that these popular training methods can be adapted to include actual wrestling as the principal activity.

To be effective in improving the athlete's stamina these following drills have to be employed in a progressive manner. They should be initiated at a relatively low level and graded so as to increase the work intensity of each practice session.

Wrestlers must be pushed a little harder each day. A man must be expected to continue to work hard after he is tired if he is to increase his capacity to keep going in actual competition. This effort will pay off for him in the third period.

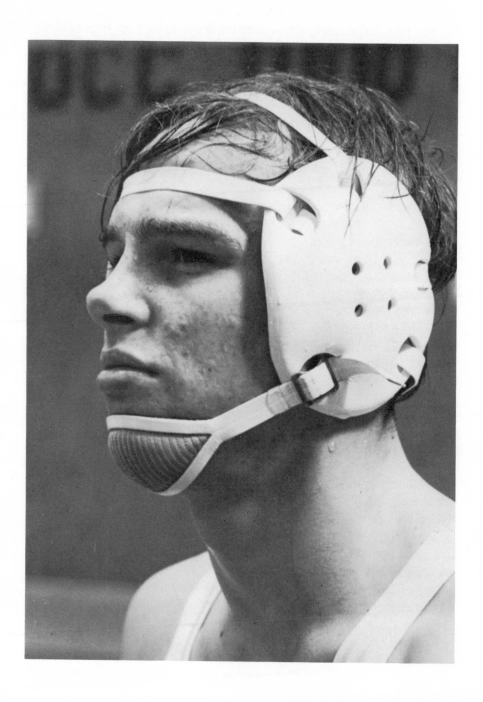

The wrestler who stops working when he gets tired will tire at this point after the same amount of effort in competition. He must drive himself past this point to improve. He must be willing to accept physical suffering and the exhausted agony that accompanies success.

There are four major variables that can be manipulated as a means of controlling the level of difficulty of each of the following drills. The variables are:

1. Duration

   The intensity of the drill can be increased by extending the time of each work interval or by increasing the number of work intervals.

2. Rest

   The work can be made more difficult by decreasing the time of each rest interval or by decreasing the number of rest intervals.

3. Pace

   The pace at which the work is performed can be increased as a means of increasing the level of difficulty of the drill.

4. Resistance

   The occasional or periodic introduction of a fresh partner can be used as a means of increasing the level of difficulty.

Since each variable can be controlled with a fair amount of accuracy, an evaluation of progress and improvement in conditioning is possible.

#71—Progressive Wrestling Drill

This drill consists of wrestling a progressively longer time with each repeated timed effort. The first few repeats are performed at a relatively low level of exertion, but then increase in intensity with each succeeding repetition. The time of each repeated rest interval is also steadily increased along with the time of each repeated effort.

Progressive Wrestling Table

Effort	Rest	Fresh Opponent	Pace
:30 sec	:10 sec	optional	match speed
:45 sec	:10 sec	”	” ”
1:00 min	:30 sec	”	” ”
1:15 min	:45 sec	”	” ”
1:30 min	:45 sec	”	” ”
1:45 min	:45 sec	”	” ”
2:00 min	1:00 min	”	” ”
2:15 min	1:00 min	”	” ”
2:30 min	1:00 min	”	” ”
2:45 min	1:00 min	”	” ”

#72—*Regressive Wrestling Drill*

Regressive wrestling entails having each successive repeated exertion preformed in a shorter interval of time than the one before. These diminishing time intervals require less of a sustained effort with each repetition.

Regressive Wrestling Table

Effort	Rest	Fresh Opponent	Pace
2:45 min	1:00 min	optional	match speed
2:30 min	1:00 min	"	" "
2:15 min	1:00 min	"	" "
2:00 min	:45 sec	"	" "
1:45 min	:45 sec	"	" "
1:30 min	:45 sec	"	" "
1:15 min	:30 sec	"	" "
1:00 min	:30 sec	"	" "
:45 sec	:10 sec	"	" "
:30 sec	:10 sec	"	" "

#73—*Alternative Wrestling Drill*

This drill alternates longer efforts with shorter ones. The duration of every other repeated effort is the same. Longer exertion periods are interspersed with shorter ones. The length of each rest interval becomes progressively longer as the drill continues and fatigue sets in.

Alternative Wrestling Table

Effort	Rest	Fresh Opponent	Pace
2:00 min	:30 sec	optional	match speed
:30 sec	:15 sec	"	" "
2:00 min	:30 sec	"	" "
:30 sec	:15 sec	"	" "
2:00 min	:45 sec	"	" "
:30 sec	:15 sec	"	" "
2:00 min	:45 sec	"	" "
:30 sec	:15 sec	"	" "
2:00 min	1:00 min	"	" "
:30 sec	:15 sec	"	" "

#74—Pyramid Wrestling Drill

The pyramid wrestling drill gets its name from the pyramiding or peaking pattern of timed efforts involved in its use. The drill is a strenuous one. No rest is allowed and a fresh opponent is repeatedly encountered for the duration of the drill.

Pyramid Wrestling Table

Effort	Rest	Fresh Opponent	Pace
3:00 min	none	B	match speed
2:30 min	"	C	" "
2:00 min	"	B	" "
1:00 min	"	C	" "
2:00 min	"	B	" "
2:30 min	"	C	" "
3:00 min	"	B	" "

Note: A wrestles with B & C alternating, then
B wrestles with A & C alternating, then
C wrestles with A & B alternating

#75—Simulator Wrestling Drill

The simulator drill simulates the effort that the wrestler must put forth in actual competition. The total time of the match is divided up into several segments. Each segment is separated by a period of rest. Any amount of time may be assigned to as many segments as desired.

Simulator Wrestling Table

Total Time Wrestling	1st Segment	Rest Interval	2nd Seg	Rest Int	3rd Seg	Rest Int	4th Int	Rest Int	5th Seg
Example A									
8:00 minutes	2:00 minutes	1:30 minutes	3:00 min	2:00 min	3:00 min				
Example B									
8:00 minutes	2:00 minutes	1:00 minutes	2:00 min	1:30 min	2:00 min.	2:00 min	2:00 min		
Example C									
minutes	minutes	sec	min	min	min	min	min	min	min
8:00	1:30	:45	1:45	1:00	1:30	1:15	1:45	1:30	1:30

#76—Straight Repetition Drill

This drill consists of a series of efforts from a neutral position, position of advantage, or defensive position. When doing a set of repeat efforts the time of each effort should be relatively constant. As the drill progresses the wrestlers are required to exert greater and greater effort.

Time of the Effort	Straight Repetition Wrestling Table Number of Repeated Efforts	Time of Rest Between Efforts
:30 seconds	32	10 to 20 sec.
1:00 minute	16	10 to 45 sec.
1:30 minutes	10	30 to 60 sec.
2:00 minutes	8	30 to 60 sec.
2:30 minutes	6	30 to 120 sec.
3:00 minutes	5	30 to 120 sec.

#77—Mixed Repetition Drill

When conducting a mixed repetition drill neither the time of the effort nor the interval of rest are constant. An example of this follows:

Mixed Repeition Wrestling Table								
Effort	1	2	3	4	5	6	7	8
Wrestling Time	3 min	2 min	2 min	4 min	1 min	2 min	1 min	1 min
Resting Time	1 min	45 sec	45 sec	2 min	30 sec	1 min	30 sec	30 sec

#78—*Fartlek Drill*

This drill incorporates elements of fartlek training. Fartlek training is a relatively unstructured mixture of various types and intensities of pace. This type of training is extremely flexible.

In general it is performed at a relatively slow speed interspersed with numerous fast-paced efforts. It can be employed as formally or as informally as desired.

A fairly rigid form of this drill is to have the men wrestle five minutes at a slow pace, three minutes at a moderate pace, and then one minute at an all-out effort. This pattern is then continuously repeated.

Fartlex Wrestling

Effort	Rest	Fresh Opponent	Pace
5 min.	none	optional	slow
3 min.	,,	,,	moderate
5 min.	,,	,,	slow
1 min.	,,	,,	all out
5 min.	,,	,,	slow
3 min.	,,	,,	moderate
5 min.	,,	,,	slow
1 min.	,,	,,	all out
5 min.	,,	,,	slow
3 min.	,,	,,	moderate
5 min.	,,	,,	slow
1 min.	,,	,,	all out
5 min.	,,	,,	slow
3 min.	,,	,,	moderate
5 min.	,,	,,	slow
1 min.	,,	,,	all out

Note: a. No rest should be allowed;
b. The inclusion of a fresh opponent is optional;
c. The slow pace provides an opportunity for practicing and correcting techniques;
The moderate pace is match speed;
The all out pace is a maximum exertion

A less formal variation of this drill is to have the team wrestle at a slow or moderate pace except for announced intervals. Such announcements are given at the coach's discretion. Then regardless of the positions the members of the team are in, they begin immediately wrestling an all-out effort until the coach again slows the pace.

The least formal and most permissive variation of this drill is to permit individual athletes to vary the pace at their own discretions. No supervision is provided. The athletes wrestle in accordance with how they feel at the moment. The only control is the amount of time this variation is practiced.

#79—Pulse-Rate Drill

This is more of an individual drill than a team drill. During the drill the wrestler attempts to elevate or maintain a certain pulse rate for a prescribed period of time. Periodically he takes a ten-second count of his pulse to determine how hard he is performing.

The drill requires wrestling a series of repeated efforts for a given time with a controlled amount of rest between each repeated effort.

The rest interval should be long enough between repeated efforts to permit partial, but not complete, recovery of the heart rate.

When counting the pulse, a watch or clock with a second hand should be kept within close view. The tips of the fingers should be moved around slightly and the pressure varied until the pulse is detected on the side of the neck. The pulse count is taken for ten seconds and then multiplied by six. The total represents the pulse beat per minute.

The higher the pulse rate the harder the wrestler is working. The sooner the heart rate recovers the better the wrestler's condition. The heart rate should be pushed to 175-180 beats per minute. The wrestler should then permit the heart to recover to 120–140 beats per minute. The heart rate should never go below 110 beats per minute during the drill.

Pulse Rate Wrestling Table

Effort	Rest	Fresh Opponent	Pace
2 min.	until pulse is between 120-140 beats per minute	B	match speed
2 min.	"	C	"
2 min.	"	B	"
2 min.	"	C	"
2 min.	"	B	"
2 min.	"	C	"
2 min.	"	B	"
2 min.	"	C	"

Note: a. At the end of each effort the pulse rate should be 175–180 beats/min. or a ten-second count of 30 beats (30 x 6 = 180).
 b. Before beginning the next effort the pulse should be between 120–140 beats/min. or a ten-second count of 20 to 23 beats.

#80—Marathon Drill

This drill employs continuous activity at a slow pace for an extended period of time. The time of the drill should be longer than that of a match.

There are two primary advantages to this drill. First, the athlete's confidence to wrestle a match without experiencing undue fatigue is enhanced as a result of having trained for extended periods of time. Second, since the pace is much slower than that of an actual match he can concentrate most his attention on perfecting techniques.

Marathon Wrestling Table
Example A

Effort	Rest	Fresh Opponent	Pace
16 min.	none	none	slower than match speed

Example B

Effort	Rest	Fresh Opponent	Pace
4 min.	none	B	slower than match speed
4 min.	"	C	"
4 min.	"	D	"
4 min.	"	E	"

#81—Sprint Drill

This drill is performed at a fast pace. Since it involves all-out efforts it should be employed with discretion.

The length of time for each all-out effort should be between thirty seconds and one minute. The drill may be conducted in an equal or unequal series of repeated efforts. The rest interval following each repeat should be long enough to allow the athlete's heart to return to something approximating its normal resting count.

Sprint Wrestling Table
Example A

Effort	Rest	Fresh Opponent	Pace
15 sec.	1 min.	optional	all-out
15 sec.	1 min.	"	" "
15 sec.	1 min.	"	" "
15 sec.	1 min.	"	" "
15 sec.	1 min.	"	" "
15 sec.	1 min.	"	" "

Example B

Effort	Rest	Fresh Opponent	Pace
45 sec.	3 min.	optional	all-out
30 sec.	2 min.	"	" "
15 sec.	1 min.	"	" "

#82—Interval Drill

This drill involves repeated efforts interspersed with recovery periods of little or no activity. It is rigidly controlled. The pace should be equal to or faster than that of a regulation match. The time of each exertion should not be greater than one and one half to three minutes. The rest interval should only be long enough for the heart rate to recover partially. It should never be longer than the time of the repeated effort. This is rarely less than thirty seconds nor in excess of three minutes.

Pulse rate is the key to determining the times of the repeat and recovery periods. Many athletes count their own pulses. When their pulse reaches 120 to 150 beats per minute the next bout should be started.

Interval Wrestling Table
Example A

Effort	Rest	Fresh Opponent	Pace	
30 sec.	½ to 1½ minutes	optional	match speed	
30 sec.	”	”	”	”
30 sec.	”	”	”	”
30 sec.	”	”	”	”
30 sec.	”	”	”	”
30 sec.	”	”	”	”
30 sec.	”	”	”	”
30 sec.	”	”	”	”
30 sec.	”	”	”	”
30 sec.	”	”	”	”

Example B

1½ min.	½ to 1½ minutes	optional	match speed	
1½ min.	”	”	”	”
1½ min.	”	”	”	”
1½ min.	”	”	”	”

#83—Repetition Drill

This drill involves bouts of fairly long duration wrestled at a relatively fast pace but with sufficient rest intervals to allow almost complete recovery of the heart rate.

Despite the fact that the pace is faster than that of a regulation match, there should be no all-out efforts. Rather the wrestler should attempt to set a tempo at which he wrestles competitively.

Repeated efforts range up to three quarters of the time of a regulation match, but never equal to or greater than that time.

The time for recovery should be at least three time greater than the time of each repeated effort. This is generally never less than one and one half minutes. The pulse should be allowed to drop to below 110 beats per minute prior to engaging in the next bout. As fatigue becomes more and more acute the length of the rest interval should be increased as the drill progresses.

Repetition Wrestling Table

Example A

Effort	Rest	Fresh Opponent	Pace
3 min.	9 to 12 minutes	optional	faster than match speed
3 min.	"	"	"
3 min.	"	"	"
3 min.	"	"	"
3 min.	"	"	"

Example B

Effort	Rest	Fresh Opponent	Pace
4 min.	12 to 15 minutes	optional	faster than match speed
4 min.	"	"	"
4 min.	"	"	"
4 min.	"	"	"

#84—Change-of-Pace Drill •

This is a change-of-pace drill. A number of different types of workouts are written up on five-by-seven cards. The cards are placed face down on a flat surface and one card is selected by each pair of wrestlers. They are expected to then go through the workout listed on the card.

Change-of-Pace Wrestling Card
This workout is to be done in the following manner:
1. Wrestle at a moderate pace until each of you gain twenty takedowns.
2. Wrestle ten two-minute efforts with a thirty-second rest between each repeated effort.
3. Wrestle three eight-minute matches with a ten-minute rest between each.

Summary
20 takedowns, then 10 x 2 repeats with 30 sec. R.I., finish with three 8 min. matches with a 10 min. rest between each.

#85—Selected Drill

The squad is paired off so every wrestler is wrestling another of approximately equal ability.

One pair of wrestlers is selected to wrestle all-out for one minute while all other pairs wrestle at half speed. After one minute they slow their pace to half speed and the coach picks another pair to begin wrestling all out. This procedure continues until all pairs have wrestled all out at least once.

Wrestling at a selected pace.

#86—All-Out Drill

This is a loosely controlled drill. The squad is paired off. The wrestlers are instructed to wrestle at their own chosen pace while reviewing
techniques. When they hear the whistle they are told to wrestle all out
until a second whistle is sounded. At the coach's discretion, an all-out
effort can be interjected at any time in the workout.

Wrestling all out.

10
RECREATIONAL DRILLS

Wrestling can become drudgery particularly during the middle and latter stages of the season. Interest begins to wade as the newness of wrestling wears off. Signs of boredom appear. While wrestlers continue to anxiously look forward to meets, they often begin to consider practice sessions as a necessary evil.

Ultimate success is largely decided by the coach's ability to maintain a high level of interest in the sport. His basic problem is making practice sessions pleasant and rewarding. However, making physical exertion fun is difficult.

The element of change helps to keep team morale and spirit high during practice sessions. A high level of interest enhances the learning environment.

Most drills can be made meaninful if a game situation is created. Gamelike drills characterized by variety and continuous motion are popular.

The best drills yield as much fun as possible. They are enjoyable while at the same time being physically challenging. The wrestlers, while participating, expend tremendous amounts of energy often without noticing their acute states of fatigue. They become so absorbed in the drill that the ordinary signs of fatigue go unnoticed.

The principal factor in making a recreational type drill successful is the coach. His pep, enthusiasm, and spirit will determine how worthwhile it is. The pace should be continuously snappy and vigorous. After a brief introduction it should be conducted with all possible immediacy.

Drills that are allowed to drag along are uninteresting and undermining to team morale. The coach should constantly stimulate the team to greater effort by exhibiting a hustling attitude combined with a spirit of enthusiasm.

The coach, from the very start, should interject motivating remarks into the drill. A constant flow of chatter should come from him in rousing enthusiasm, stimulating the spirit of competition, and keeping things alive. Spirited words help to stimulate interest.

The wrestlers that are losing should be given encouragement. The winning wrestlers do not need such encouragement since being ahead provides all that is necessary. Occassionally, the coach can stimulate a losing side by joining them.

#87—Charge Drill

This game-type drill gets its name from the frequent use of the word *charge*. It begins by either choosing up sides or dividing the team into two groups.

The coach assigns one group a task. The other group is told to prevent it. Examples of tasks are as follows:

1. The members of one group are told to remain standing on their feet. The other group is given the task of taking them down and keeping them from regaining a standing position.

2. One group is told to remain prone while the other is told to get them turned over onto their backs and hold them there.

3. One group is told to maintain at least some part of their bodies in contact with a line on the mat while the other group is to prevent this action.

At the conclusion of the assigned task each player is instructed to remain in his last position in order to be counted. Scores are totalled at the end of the task.

The roles of each group are then reversed. In this way each group has to accomplish and prevent the same tasks.

The number of tasks that can be assigned is only limited by the coach's imagination and creativity.

Charging the opposing team.

#88—Fortress Drill

The team is divided into two groups of approximately equal size and ability.

A volleyball or basketball is placed in the center of the mat. One team, the defending one, forms a circle facing away from the ball.

The opposing team attempts to penetrate the circle, grab the ball, and carry it out of the circle as quickly as possible.

When either the ball is successfully carried from the circle or the two-minute time limit has expired, the attacking and defending teams exchange roles. After a predetermined number of rounds the team having the smallest accumulative time is the winner.

The defending team may not touch the ball although it is allowed to prevent members of the opposing team from leaving the circle with the ball.

Defending the fortress.

#89—Steal-the-Bacon Drill

All wrestlers are paired off according to weight and told to line up along one side of the room. The coach starts at one end of the line and assigns each pair of wrestlers a single number.

Members of each pair, having identical numbers, take up positions facing each other on opposite sides of the mat.

A volleyball is placed in the center of the mat between the two groups of wrestlers. The objective of the game is to carry the ball back over the wrestler's own boundary line when his number is called.

The coach calls out any number or series of numbers. Those wrestlers rush out and grab for the ball. Any wrestler carrying the ball across his own boundary line scores one point for his team.

The coach should inform the teams that no number will be called for those wrestlers who allow their feet to extend over the limit line. No points will be scored unless the ball or the wrestler holding the ball is carried over the line. The ball may not be kicked or thrown across the line. Players whose numbers have not been called may not assist in getting the ball across their line.

Attempting to secure control of the ball.

#90—Flag Drill

Each wrestler is given a set of clip-on flags and a belt commonly used in the game of flag football. If flag sets are not available, ten-by-two strips of cloth can be substituted.

All wrestlers are told to scatter out around the perimeter of the mat. Each wrestler is on his own.

The objective, on the whistle, is to remove and collect as many of the other player's flags as possible.

No wrestler is allowed to touch his own flags as a means of protecting them. Once he has lost both his flags he must sit down. The drill continues until only one wrestler has any flags. At that time the wrestler having collected the most flags is declared the winner.

The drill is an excellent means of practicing stance, footwork, and defending against leg takedowns.

Attempting to remove flags.

#91—Black-Mark Drill

This is an excellent intrasquad drill. The team lines up along the wall with the lightest man at one end to the heaviest man at the other end of the line. The coach then has them count off by fours. Each group of four represents a weight class. The members of each weight class compete in the following round-robin fashion.

Wrestler		*Wrestler*
1	vs.	2
3	vs.	4
1	vs.	4
2	vs.	3
1	vs.	3
4	vs.	2

To determine the winner of each weight class, a bad-mark system of points is used. The boy who has the fewest number of bad points is declared the winner of each weight class.

Each match consists of three one-minute periods similar to a regulation match. Bad points are scored as follows:

Winner by a fall .... 0 bad points
Winner by points .... 1 bad point
Draw .... 2 bad points
Loser by points .... 3 bad points
Loser by a fall .... 4 bad points

#92—Bad-Point Takedown Drill

The team lines up in a single file according to weight and counts off by threes. Each group of three represents a weight class. Each boy wrestles every other boy in his group.

Wrestler		Wrestler
1	vs.	2
2	vs.	3
1	vs.	3

The objective is to get takedowns while not being taken down. All wrestling is done from the neutral position. Wrestling is stopped after each takedown so the wrestlers can begin again standing. The match winner is the wrestler who is the first to gain two takedowns within three minutes. The overall winner is the wrestler with the lowest total number of bad points according to the following table:

		Bad Points	
Wrestler #1	Wrestler #2	#1	#2
Zero takedowns	Zero takedowns	2	2
One takedown	Zero takedowns	1	3
One takedown	One takedown	2	2
Two takedowns	One takedown	1	3
Two takedowns	Zero takedown	0	4

#93—Ten-Point Drill

The squad is divided into two equally talented teams. Members from each team then compete in an intrasquad meet. The rules are as follows:

1. A fall at any time ends the match and the winning wrestler gets ten points for his team. The points earned by the loser are added to his team's total score.
2. The match ends when either wrestler earns ten points. The loser's points are added to his team's total score.
3. If the match ends before a fall occurs or either wrestler scores ten points, then each wrestler's points are added to his team's total score.

This drill encourages the boy who is losing from giving up before the match ends.

Competing for points.

#94—Intrasquad Drill

This drill is especially popular during vacation periods and long intervals of time between meets.

The team is divided into two squads. The squads are selected in such a manner as to be as equal in ability as possible. To stimulate interest in the drill the head coach can take charge of one squad while his assistant takes over the other. Interest can further be increased by having the losing coach and squad pay a penalty such as running X number of laps or climbing stadium stairs.

The drill is conducted the same as any regulation meet. If the team is exceptionally large, three or four squads can be selected to compete.

Wrestlers earn points for their teams by winning. The team with the highest number of earned points at the end of the drill is declared the winner.

Wrestling an intrasquad meet.

#95—Free-Wrestling Drill

The activity of wrestling is itself fun and exciting. It is much more enjoyable than the routine of practicing techniques.

For a change of pace provisions should be made to include simple "wrasslin" in workouts. It consists basically "rolling around on the mat."

This provides a very relaxed environment void of the usual pressures characteristic of the more formally regulated workouts. It provides an excellent opportunity for wrestlers to work on the finer points of favored techniques. Newly learned moves and older ones can be perfected.

There are no time limits, with everything being loosely organized. The wrestlers may change partners at will. They are free to stop and advise each other on proper movements and refer any problems or questions to the coach who is rotating among them. They may wrestle at any pace desired.

Wrestling at an informal pace.

#96—Near-Fall and Fall Drill

The team is divided into two squads. A regulation meet is conducted. However, only near-falls and falls are counted. No points are awarded for takedowns, escapes, reversals, or riding time. Team scores are kept.

To encourage aggressiveness more points are awarded for earlier near-falls and falls. The system of scoring is as follows:

	Points Scored	
Period	Near-Fall	Fall
1st	3	6
2nd	2	5
3rd	1	4

Being able to secure a near-fall or fall early in the match is highlighted in this method of scoring.

Working for a fall.

#97—Touch-Thigh Drill

The wrestlers pair off by weight. The drill is performed entirely in a neutral standing position. The objective is to touch or slap the opponent's thigh or knee. It is assumed that if a wrestler is able to make contact with his opponent's thigh, he would normally be able to secure a takedown.

Beginning position standing.

#98—Line Drill

All the wrestlers are divided into two evenly matched groups. Both groups start on opposite sides of the mat facing each other. Some means of distinguishing the groups, such as shirts and no shirts, should be provided.

On the whistle all wrestlers go toward the center of the mat and attempt to push, pull, lift, or carry any opposing wrestler across their own goal line.

Any wrestler forced across an opponent's goal line is eliminated from the competition. The drill continues until only one side has wrestlers remaining in competition.

Competing to win.

#99—Tag-Team Drill

The team lines up along the wall from the lowest weight to the highest weight. Starting with the lowest weight the wrestlers count off by fours. Each group of four represents two pairs of wrestlers. Each group is assigned a portion of the mat.

One wrestler from each pair is placed in the center of his respective portion of the mat. On the signal they begin to wrestle. At any time one of the wrestlers touches his teammate who is on the sideline, his teammate comes on to the mat and replaces him. The wrestler who did the tagging must leave the mat as quickly as possible.

Teammates are allowed to stand at the edge of the mat to be tagged. They must, however, remain on their side of the mat and may not have any portion of their body touching the mat proper.

To insure fairness, those wrestlers not competing should act as referees and scorekeepers.

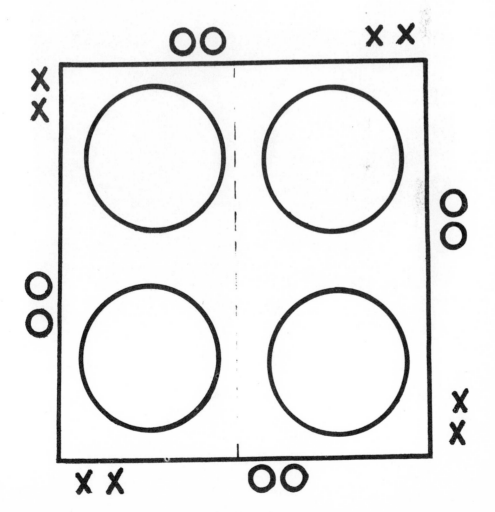

#100—Circle Drill

This drill stresses holddowns.

Divide the team into evenly matched groups. Since there will be a mingling of wrestlers, one group should either wear anklets or remove their shirts. Unless this is done, groups will unknowingly compete against themselves.

One group begins in a standing position within the mat circle. At the signal the other group attempts to force or throw the first group out of the circle and hold them out.

All tactics are fair except unnecessary roughness and illegal holds. After two minutes the whistle is blown and every player remains motionless while being counted. Any wrestler from the group, which originally started in the circle, who has any part of his body inside the ring scores one point for his side. The groups then change positions.

Forcing wrestlers from the circle.

#101—Pin Drill

Two groups of evenly matched wrestlers assume positions on opposite sides of the mat. The members of one group are identified from the other group by wearing anklets or removing their shirts.

All wrestlers start on their hands and knees. No one is allowed to stand up during the drill. On the whistle the wrestlers crawl toward their opponents. The objective is to hold an opponent's shoulders to the mat momentarily. The coach eliminates those who get pinned. The winners continue and may assist teammates in pinning other opponents. The drill ends after three minutes or when there are only members of one group left on the mat.

Attempting to pin.

BIBLIOGRAPHY

Benjamin, Lloyd. "Middle School Wrestling Program." *The Coaching Clinic* (September 1967): pp. 25–28.

Borkowski, Richard P. "An Obstacle Course-Wrestling Style." *Scholastic Wrestling News* (December 15, 1972): pp. 28–29.

Borkowski, Richard P., and Dayton, Andrew I. "Rough and Tumble." *Journal of Health, Physical Education, and Recreation* (April 1967: pp. 28–31.

Brown, Robert L., and Ober, D. Kenneth. *Complete Book of High School Wrestling.* Englewood Cliffs, N.J.: Prentice-Hall, Inc., 1962.

Brown, Robert L., and Robertson, Thomas E. *Illustrated Guide to the Takedown in Wrestling.* West Nyack, N.Y.: Parker Publishing Co., Inc., 1967.

Camaione, David N., and Tillman, Kenneth G. *Wrestling Methods.* New York: The Ronald Press Co., 1968.

Carson, Ray F. *Championship Wrestling: Coaching To Win.* South Brunswick, N.J.: A. S. Barnes and Co., Inc., 1974.

————. "Evaluating Wrestling Effort." *Scholastic Coach* (March 1971): pp. 86–87.

————. "Interval Circuit Wrestling." *Scholastic Coach* (April 1971): p. 37.

Carson, Ray F., and Patterson, Buel R. *Principles of Championship Wrestling.* South Brunswick, N.J.: A. S. Barnes and Co., Inc., 1972.

Carson, Raymond F., Jr. *Systematic Championship Wrestling.* South Brunswick, N.J.: A. S. Barnes and Co., Inc., 1972.

Clayton, Thompson. *A Handbook of Wrestling Terms and Holds.* South Brunswick, N.J.: A. S. Barnes and Co., Inc., 1968.

Collins, Richard K. "Wrestling Drills for Conditioning and Skill Development." *The Coaching Clinic* (August 1970): pp. 10–11.

Corder, Bill. "A Conditioning Program for High School Wrestling." *The Coaching Clinic* (October 1968): pp. 26–27.

Counsilman, James E. *The Science of Swimming.* Englewood Cliffs, N.J.: Prentice-Hall, Inc., 1968.

Crockett, David S. "Complete Drill Program for High School Wrestlers." *Scholastic Coach* (January 1961): pp. 82–84.

————. Escape and Reversal Series for High School Wrestlers." *Scholastic Coach* (October 1962): p. 28.

Daher, Joseph G. "Methods and Techniques of Teaching Wrestling." *The Athletic Journal* (November 1946): pp. 12–15.

Dannehl, Wayne E. "College Wrestling—The Big Bore." *Coach and Athlete* (May 1969): p. 20.

Douglas, Bob. *Wrestling: The Making of a Champion.* Ithaca, N.Y.: Cornell University Press, 1972.

Dratz, John P., Johnson, Manly, and McCann, Terry. *Winning Wrestling.* Englewood Cliffs, N.J.: Prentice-Hall, Inc., 1966.

Elliott, Ed M. "Wrestling for Limited Areas." *The Athletic Journal* (October 1970): p. 10.

Gallagher, Ed C. *Wrestling.* New York: A. S. Barnes and Co., 1939.

Gallagher, Ed C., and Perry, Rex. *Wrestling.* New York: The Ronald Press Co., 1951.

Gardner, Frank. *Wrestling.* New York: Thomas Nelson and Sons, 1963.

Gianakaris, George. *Action Drilling in Wrestling.* South Brunswick, N.Y.: A.S. Barnes and Co., Inc., 1969.

————. "Full Squad Wrestling Drills." *The Athletic Journal* (November 1967): pp. 54–55.

Griffith, Art. "Griffith's Scoring System for Dual Matches." Typed papers distributed by the author.

Halverson, Robert. "Chain Wrestling Drills." *The Coaching Clinic* (July 1971): pp. 23–23.

Hanke, Al. "Continuous Movement and Situation Drills in Wrestling." *The Athletic Journal* (December 1963): pp. 26–27.

Harrison, E. J. *Wrestling.* New York. W. Foulsham and Co., Ltd., 1960.

Hunt, Briggs. *Greco-Roman Wrestling.* New York: The Ronald Press Co., 1964.

————. "Let's Give Wrestling the Break It Deserves." *Scholastic Wrestling News* (December 15, 1969): p. 19.

Johnson, Neil R. "Simplicity and Drill." *Scholastic Coach* (December 1966): pp. 32–33.

Kapral, Frank. *Coach's Illustrated Guide to Championship Wrestling.* Englewood Cliffs, N.J.: Prentice-Hall, Inc. 1964.

Keen, Cliff, Speidal, Charles, and Swartz, Ray. *Championship Wrestling.* Annapolis: U. S. Naval Institute, 1964.

Keith, Art. *Complete Guide to Championship Wrestling.* West Nyack, N.Y.: Parker Publishing Co., Inc., 1968.

Keller, Neil. *"Wrestling Practice:* Ideas and Techniques." *The Coaching Clinic* (August 1969): pp. 18–22.

Kenney, Harold E., and Law, Glenn. *Wrestling.* New York: McGraw-Hill Co., 1952.

Lantz, Everett D. *Wrestling Guide.* Laramie, Wyoming: The Midwest Sporting Goods, Inc., 1960.

Levine, Howard. "Incentive Devices in Small School Wrestling." *The Athletic Journal* (September 1968): pp. 82–83.

Leyshon, Glynn A. "Handicapped Wrestling Practice." *Scholastic Coach* (January 1968): p. 46.

Littlefield, Henry M. "Circular Drills." *Scholastic Wrestling News* (October 15, 1972): pp. 7–10.

Lorence, Robert C. "Wrestling Drills and Workout Plans." *The Athletic Journal* (October 1968): pp. 84–87.

Macias, Rummy. *Learning How Wrestling.* Mankato, Minnesota: Creative Educational Society, 1964.

Maertz, Richard C. *Wrestling Teaching Guide.* South Brunswick, N.J.: A. S. Barnes and Co., Inc., 1972.

————. *Wrestling Techniques: Takedowns.* South Brunswick, N.J.: A. S. Barnes and Co., Inc., 1970.

Mann, William C. "Series Versus Individual Techniques in Wrestling Instruction." *The Athletic Journal* (November 1957): pp. 46–47.

Martin, George. *The Mechanics of Wrestling.* Madison, Wisconsin: College Printing and Typing Co., 1962.

Masek, Melvin L. "Quick Hands Drill." *Scholastic Wrestling News* (January 15, 1970): p. 17.

Meyers, Edward J. *A Programmed Guide to Wrestling Rules.* Veron, Conn.: Verson Publishers, 1971.

Moretz, V. J. "New Scoring for an Old Sport, Wrestling." *The Athletic Journal* (May 1962): p. 34.

Parker, Charles W., ed. *The Official N.C.A.A. Wrestling Guide.* Phoenix, Ariz.: College Athletics Publishing Service, 1973.

Peery, Rex, and Umbach, Arnold. *How To Improve Your Wrestling.* Chicago: The Athletic Institute, 1958.

Rash, Philip J., and Kroll, Warren. *What Research Tells the Coach about Wrestling.* Washington D.C.: American Association for Health, Physical Education and Recreation, 1964.

Sasahara, Shozo. *Fundamentals of Scientific Wrestling.* Japan: Chuo University Co-Operation Press, 1960.

Sarratt, M. T. "Ten Questions for the Novice Wrestling Coach." *The Athletic Journal* (October 1970): p. 32.

Smith, James A. "Pins Are In." *Coach and Athlete* (February 1971): p. 16.

Sparks, Raymond E. "Mat Drills." *Journal of Health, Physical Education and Recreation* (December 1956): pp. 42–43.

————. *Wrestling Illustrated.* New York: The Ronald Press Co., 1960.

Staley, Seward C. *Games, Contests, and Relays.* New York: A. S. Barnes and Co., 1924.

Stinle, Harlan. "Blind Man Drill." *Scholastic Wrestling News* (March 15, 1970): p. 12.

Stone, Henry A. *Wrestling: Intercollegiate and Olympic.* New York: Prentice-Hall, Inc., 1945.

Stehlow, Roland. "Wrestling Situation Drills." *Scholastic Coach* (March 1971): p. 66.

Swalec, John J. "Takedown Drills." *Scholastic Coach* (June 1968): p. 36.

Talamo, Joe, and Lupinacci, Roy. *Developing a Championship Football Program.* West Nyack, N.Y.: Parker Publishing Co., Inc., 1968.

Tillman, Kenneth, and Keefe, Dick. "The Whizzer Wheel." *The Athletic Journal* (January 1973): p. 10—11.

Umbach, Arnold, and Johnson, Warren. *Successful Wrestling.* Dubuque, Iowa: Wililam C. Brown Co., 1960

Valentine, Tom. *Inside Wrestling.* Chicago: Henry Regnery Co., 1972.

Weiss, Steven A. "Early Season Wrestling Drills." *The Coaching Clinic* (July 1967): pp. 29–31.

———. "Organize Your Wrestling Workouts." *The Athletic Journal* (September 1970): pp. 92–95.

———. "Takedown Setups." *The Athletic Journal* (November 1968): p. 38.

Yahr, Don. "Winning Wrestling Drills." *The Coaching Clinic* (October 1967): pp. 13–15.

Yuhasz, Mike, Leyshon. Glynn, and Salter, Bill. *Basic Wrestling.* Ontario: The University of Western Ontario Press, 1963.